SCOTTISH JOURNAL OF THEOLOGY

Current Issues in Theology

Edited by
IAIN TORRANCE

SCOTTISH JOURNAL OF THEOLOGY

Current Issues in Theology

Edited by

IAIN TORRANCE

This is a series of short books specially commissioned by the editor of *Scottish Journal of Theology*. The aim is to commission books which stand between the static monograph genre and the more immediate statement of a journal article. Following the long tradition of the *Journal*, the editor will commission authors who are questioning existing paradigms or rethinking perspectives. It is hoped that the books will appeal to a wide range of readers.

Believing that living theology needs an audience and thrives on debate, the editor will invite the authors to present the themes of their topics in four public lectures at the University of Aberdeen (*The Scottish Journal of Theology Lectures*), and the books, which will be published subsequently, will be developed from these.

The *Scottish Journal of Theology* is an international refereed quarterly journal of systematic, historical and biblical theology published by T&T Clark Ltd, 59 George Street, Edinburgh EH2 2LQ, Scotland. Subscription details are available on request from the Publishers.

PROPHECY AND MYSTICISM

To my students both from Feminisme en Christendom *at the Catholic University of Nijmegen, The Netherlands, and at La Sainte Union College, Southampton, Great Britain, whose prophetic words, creativity and expressions of community continue to provide wellsprings of hope.*

PROPHECY AND MYSTICISM

The Heart of the Postmodern Church

MARY C. GREY

T&T CLARK
EDINBURGH

T&T CLARK LTD
59 GEORGE STREET
EDINBURGH EH2 2LQ
SCOTLAND

First published 1997

ISBN 0 567 08587 2

British Library Cataloguing-in-Publication Data
A catalogue record for this book is available from the British Library

Typeset by Waverley Typesetters, Galashiels
Printed and bound in Great Britain by Page Bros, Norwich

Contents

Introduction

It is certainly not original to relate contemporary problems in society to the victory of a rampant individualism. I am very aware that to broach the topic in Scotland, where Mrs Thatcher made her famous statement that 'there is no such thing as society', is to tread on dynamite. To be an individual – according to the current wisdom – it is vital to compete and to succeed. To succeed one has to be a consumer. The cult of money, of an overwhelming consumerism, has crept into the very definition of our postmodern identity, so that 'I shop, I spend, therefore I am' (*Tesco, ergo sum,* according to one wit!) is now a more authentic expression of identity than the 'cogito ergo sum' of René Descartes. Secondly, there is awareness of the gravity of a crisis of values, where ten-year-olds are capable of violence and even murder, and schools struggle to stay open with a rising level of violent pupils, but on the eve of a general election, strange to relate(!), it is the politicians rather than church leaders who are trying to seize the moral high ground. Yet they do this against a background where, we are told, the grand universal stories are no more, 'the centre does not hold', and, recalling Yeats's words, we are fairly near to 'mere anarchy [being] loosed upon the world'.[1] And this is occurring at a time when, partly as a result of the erosion of democracy following their policies, the very notion of community seems to be in fragments. Whether we speak of school, family or Church, or

[1] W. B. Yeats, 'The Second Coming', in *Poems,* Variorum edn. (New York: Macmillan, reprinted 1973), p. 402.

1

the village as a cohesive social unity, what we see is fragmentation on a global scale.[2]

Against this bleak scenario, this book reflects on what mysticism and prophecy might mean today. I argue that the days of the angry prophet of the Hebrew Scriptures as individual, together with the image of the levitating mystic – and their counterparts in other cultures – have had their day; what is needed is *the community as prophet*. But to be *prophetic*, I argue, is inseparable from being a *mystical* community. To understand the crucial importance of these two dimensions and their interrelatedness, I begin by entering into a dialogue with the late Thomas Merton, a Trappist monk whose reputation and influence still grow, twenty-eight years now after his death.[3] I place some key ideas of Merton's in tension with insights from Feminist Theology – insights which will be developed in chapter 3, 'The Dark Night of the Church'. In chapter 2, I explore the roots of a theology which will build a more integrated notion of community; this integral notion is linked with the recognition that God, too, is vulnerable and that communities are empowered by taking vulnerability – God's and their own – as the foundation of our communal existence. Chapter 3 discusses the 'Dark Night of the Church' as the place where we are at the moment; I argue that only the community which is true to its mystical and prophetic heart can develop the transformative capacity which a fragmented society needs. Finally, in chapter 4, I ask both what kind of prophetic action is necessary for the transformation of society and what revelation of the Spirit/ruaḥ of God will refuel the prophetic heart of community.

---

[2] There are exceptions to this: I know, for example, that in the wake of the Dunblane tragedy a powerful expression of community of sympathy was awakened, in Dunblane, throughout Scotland, and far beyond; the tangible consequence is the Snowdrop Campaign, which still arouses opposition in a society obstinately attached to the violence of a gun culture.

[3] An earlier form of what follows can be found in M. Grey, 'Escape the World or Change the World? Towards a Feminist Theology of Contemplation' in *Your Heart is my Hermitage: Thomas Merton's Vision of Solitude and Community* (Thomas Merton Society of Great Britain and Ireland, London, 1996), pp. 48–59.

This project arises from a book I have just finished, *Beyond the Dark Night – A Theology of Church*;[4] working on key dimensions of Church for today, I found myself falling back again and again on the conviction that somehow, mysticism and prophecy had to be recovered by ordinary people in community as a countercultural alternative to the death-dealing forces of much of contemporary living. I remain grateful that the opportunity to give the *Scottish Journal of Theology* Lectures in December 1996 allowed me to develop the project further.

[4] Forthcoming (London: Geoffrey Chapman, 1997).

I

Escape the world
or change the world?

*A dialogue between Feminist Theology
and Thomas Merton*

Introduction

Our own particular crisis has its roots in the cultural despair which followed the initial euphoria at the fall of Communism in the Eastern European countries. Nothing, it seems, will check the advance of unbridled capitalism. Yet the break-up of the old theological certainties might be said to go back to the conviction that, after the Second World War, nothing could be the same: God had died in Auschwitz. Paul Tillich's idea of the 'Shaking of the Foundations' seems in retrospect to be already prophetic of the end of modernity.[1] It seems that we have no spiritual or moral resources with which to stem the flood of violent conflicts that have been set in motion. Nor is religion guiltless as regards the phenomenon of the unstoppable consumerism which I mentioned in my introduction. A culture of consumerism can all too easily permeate or be assimilated by our rituals and religious festivals. As a recent book, *Consumer Rites: the Buying and Selling of American Holidays*, pointed out:

[1] See Paul Tillich, *The Shaking of the Foundations* (London: Pelican, 1962); I have developed this idea in M. Grey, 'The Shaking of the Foundations – Again! Culture and the Liberation of Theology' in *Louvain Studies* 20 (1995), pp. 347–61.

> In the United States, religion and religious leaders have pioneered
> to an extraordinary degree in the invention of marketing techniques
> that have shaped the rhythms of consumer buying habits . . . the
> shopping mall has become the central location for the commemora-
> tion of Christianity's most important holy days as well as for the
> enactment of America's most prominent civic holidays.[2]

If we add to this bleak picture the disillusionment following the
breakdown of peace movements and peace processes and the seem-
ingly unstoppable rate at which the ravaging of the environment
increases, it is small wonder that 'a culture of fragments' describes
our impasse.

Feminist theologians have particular reasons for reaching a
sense of cultural despair. It is not just the simple fact of burn-out
which we share with all activists whose movements have lost
their charge. It is not just that violence against women is increasing.
It is a combination of these with the fact that just as we were
about to reach a crucial moment in our work, and see the global
inter-connections between sexism, racism, economic poverty and
militarism, a cultural assumption has developed that feminism as a
movement is passé, the battle is won, and there is a fierce and deadly
backlash against even using the word.

So it is not out of a conviction that political action is finished
or pointless and that now is the time to sink into self-indulgent
consumerism, that I seek to develop a feminist theology of contemplation. I seek it here, in the context of this book, as the
means to the recovery of community, and in order to find a way of
staying with the struggle and re-source it in a way that frees new
energy for gathering and re-shaping the cultural fragments. The
notion of the God who is our passion for justice has inspired and
fuelled many of us in the last ten years.[3] Perhaps there are new

---

[2] Leigh Eric Schmidt, *Consumer Rites: the Buying and Selling of American
Holidays* (Princeton University Press, 1996). The quotation is from 'Mall things
bright and beautiful', a review of Schmidt's book by R. Laurence Moore in
The Times Higher Education Supplement, London, 29 March 1996, p. 22.

[3] See Carter Heyward, *Our Passion for Justice* (New York: Pilgrim, 1984);
M. Grey, *Redeeming the Dream: Feminism, Redemption and Christianity* (London:
SPCK, 1989).

embodiments of divine power in our midst to be discovered by the honest admission of our failures, the limits of our finitude, our anguish at the rejection of our visions of truth and justice. And even if there is no great vision awaiting, simply to find courage to stay in the struggle will justify this search.

But why Thomas Merton as a dialogue partner? I encountered his spell many years ago through the English version of his auto-biography *Elected Silence*,[4] with its introduction by Evelyn Waugh. But I had already been enchanted by the story of the monastery of Gethsemane through an earlier work by a fellow-Cistercian, *Burnt-out Incense*, which told of the monastery's foundation.[5] It coincided with my very romantic, idealised attachment to religion, the kind which the later Merton scorned. Escaping the world, detachment from worldly goods – not that I had any! – punishing the body (I remember my sisters and I tried to build a bed of nails in imitation of St Rose of Lima!) – all this seemed of the utmost importance. It was a typical outlook of a Roman Catholic childhood of this period and many of these early pretentions to sanctity were, fortunately, knocked out of me by the rough and tumble of living. But years of activism and struggle in various justice movements have brought me full circle. Not the romance of 'burnt-out incense' but sheer burn-out, plain and simple, has driven me back to Merton, but with a completely different motivation, namely, seeking a way out of the dark night of despair. This is not a despair that stems from personal hopelessness, but one which focuses on Christian community.

Another catalyst has been the recent publication of the corres-pondence between Professor Rosemary Radford Ruether and Thomas Merton.[6] This – as many readers will know – is a very poignant exchange between the young Rosemary Ruether, just beginning her career, and Merton, who, one year before he died, is

---

[4] Thomas Merton, *Elected Silence* (London: Hollis & Carter, 1949).

[5] M. Raymond OCSO, *Burnt-out Incense* (New York: P. J. Kennedy & Sons, 1949).

[6] *At Home in the World: The Letters of Thomas Merton and Rosemary Radford Ruether*, ed. Mary Tardiff OP, introduced by Rosemary Ruether (Maryknoll: Orbis, 1995).

struggling for further authenticity in his monastic vocation and to understand his place in the Church: he cries,

> I do wonder at times if the Church is real at all . . . Am I part of a great big hoax?[7]

The intensity of the letters focuses on the issue of whether monasticism is really about escaping the world; or more specifically, how can it be considered as a response to the wretchedness of the inner cities, a wretchedness which demands a real commitment of anyone who takes the kingdom seriously. As Ruether insists:

> For those who wish to be at the 'kingdom' frontier of history, it is the steaming ghetto of my big city, not the countryside that is the place of the radical overcoming of this world, the place where one renews creation.[8]

She argues vigorously that – recalling Plato's myth of the Cave – one has to go back to release those who are imprisoned within, and questions the authenticity of a contemplation which is out of relation with touch, sight, smell, verbal feel of another.

Merton's reply is a spirited defence of monasticism's part of the total vocation of the Church, which he insists is living a life of total integration with creation. Referring to the thousands of pine saplings which he and his novices have planted, he argues that

> the monk is one of those who not only saves the world in a theological sense, but saves it literally, protecting it against the destructiveness of the rampaging city of greed, war, etc.[9]

But Ruether will not have it. The *shalom* of the kingdom – lions lying down with lambs – will only be realised through historical redemption, through 'struggling with the powers and principalities where they really are', not by taking off into the hills! (p. 41) It will be a result of taking seriously the injunction to 'stay hooked into and love the world of technology'.[10]

---

[7] Ibid., p. 17.
[8] Ibid., p. 20.
[9] Ibid., p. 35.
[10] Ibid., p. 41.

It is striking that Merton's spirited reply – 'Is there anything you can do in the city to stop the war in Vietnam?' (p. 43) – is an indication of how deep over the years had become his commitment to peace and social justice, and how clearly he repudiated his earlier quite clear rejection of the world.

The point I am developing here is that now, twenty-eight years later, Rosemary Ruether, although radically involved in the struggle against multiple interlocking oppressions, is also a pioneer in ecological theology (which she lives out in a variety of ways, including gardening) and Merton's own inspiration of the Peace Movement and social justice generally has developed greatly over the years since his death. So this nodal point of tension (escape the world or change the world? Mysticism *or* activism?), which proves to be a *false* dichotomy in the case of Ruether and Merton, I take as jumping-off point for my explorations.

Returning to the Dark Night: only a mystical faith will save us now?

It is no surprise that, across many denominations of Christianity, a return to mystical faith is being witnessed in different ways. There is a hunger for the prayer of silence and meditation, great enthusiasm for medieval mystics like Hildegarde of Bingen (who has made it to the charts!), Teresa of Avila and John of the Cross, and through the alliance between creation spirituality and new cosmology this has led to many people rediscovering the immanence of God in creation. Furthermore, many religious congregations are discovering new contextual meanings for the original mystical charism of their founder/foundress.[11] Distrust of mere verbiage and the wordy character of liturgies, together with a rejection of theology as merely a cerebral activity which does not touch the whole person, has stimulated the recovery of what I call *theologia*, the mystical theology of the early Church. The very

[11] An important example of this is the doctoral study of Sister Myra Poole, *Standing Again at Compiègne*, which is a re-examination of the mysticism of St Julie Billiart in the light of contemporary feminist spirituality.

climate of postmodernism itself, in its challenge to timeless, de-contextualised dogmatic expressions of 'universal truth', has encouraged the return of the *Via Negativa*, the apophatic way of darkness and unknowing.

But it is vital to look at the context where this is occurring. Mystical insights, as Grace Jantzen writes in her new book *Power, Gender and Christian Mysticism*,[12] do not free-float through history, but are in direct response to the needs of the times. Thus Julian of Norwich wrote down her visions when the Black Death was sweeping across Europe; John of the Cross described his way of the Dark Night when he was literally in a Spanish prison, persecuted by his own order. It seems that the consciousness of being in crisis, of reaching the end of known solutions, can create a receptivity and openness to God's search for us. But surely this is not properly the activity of an individual, or one stemming from the eccentricity of certain individuals? Grace Jantzen accuses William James of shrinking mysticism to the private experience of an individual characterised by ineffability.[13] Likewise Denys Turner, in his study *The Darkness of God*, is scornful of the very idea of 'mystical experience'.[14] Rather, mysticism is properly related to a community's struggle; and what seems particularly to characterise the mystics is the desire to communicate God's revelation, always within the humble consciousness that language is a poor vehicle. So the hunger for a mystical and contemplative faith is not the *private* search for comfort in the experience of lostness and current confusion; it springs from the existential angst of our time, from the struggle against despair and the determination to keep hope alive.

[12] Grace M. Jantzen, *Power, Gender and Mysticism* (CUP, 1995).

[13] Jantzen, op. cit., pp. 304–7. She cites James on ineffability: 'The handiest of marks by which I classify a state of mind as mystical is negative. The subject of it immediately says that it defies expression, that no adequate report of its contents can be given in words . . . In this peculiarity, mystical states are more like states of feeling than like states of intellect' (James, *The Varieties of Religious Experience: the Gifford Lectures of 1901–2* [Collins: Glasgow, 1960, p. 367]).

[14] Denys Turner, *The Darkness of God: Negativity in Christian Mysticism* (CUP, 1995).

But it is not only the plight of the present which is the catalyst for the search for the recovery of mysticism. There is a nodal point at the heart of Feminist Theology which encounters mystical faith and touches the heart of Merton's own concerns. First, there is a concentration on the search for self, through a process of stripping off layers of false and illusory selves. Secondly, there is a search for God, beyond the limits of the traditional concepts to an understanding of dependence which respects human freedom and autonomy.[15] And, thirdly, there is a search for life in all its fullness, through what Mary Daly called a 'biophilic' (life-giving) analysis, as opposed to the social structures of patriarchy, which are by definition necrophilic or death-dealing. It is because Merton saw the contemplative life as fullness – 'contemplation is life itself, fully awake, fully alive, fully aware that it is alive'[16] – that I justify the congruence between his thought and the feminist theological insights I develop as part of this project of recovering community.

Can a feminist walk the path of kenosis?

Before exploring these three points, it is crucial to state that the starting points of Merton and Feminist Theology are very different. That was made very clear by the tensions I discussed between the priorities of Ruether and Merton as seen in the correspondence. Feminism is rooted in the desire for justice for women. Even if there are many types of feminism and strands within them,[17] the binding common core is the disordered pattern of relating between women, men and the non-human world, which is bred by the structure of patriarchy (kyriarchy). The tension between world-affirming/world-denying which was

[15] This is the theme of Sarah Coakley, *The Three-personed God: An Exploration in Théologie totale* (The Hulsean Lectures 1992; CUP forthcoming).

[16] From *New Seeds of Contemplation*, cited in William H. Shannon, *Thomas Merton's Dark Path* (Farrar, Straus & Giroux, revised edn., 1987), p. 150.

[17] See the discussion in Maria Riley, *Transforming Feminism* (Kansas City: Sheed & Ward, 1989), of liberal, romantic, radical and separatist feminism; Linda Hogan, *From Women's Experience to Feminist Theology* (Sheffield Academic Press, 1995).

such a stumbling block for the early Merton does not exist in the same way in feminism. Rather, women struggle to be given a place in the world, a place in the structures other than simply being the *other*, the reflection and mirror image of the least desirable or rejected parts of the male personality. If there is a hermeneutical priority for Feminist Theology it is that the needs of poor women are to be placed first. At the Costa Rica Dialogue of women theologians from South and North, where I coordinated the European contribution, this was exactly our priority;[18] 'If it's good for poor women it's good for all' is a slogan already preferred by black and Hispanic communities. This echoes the 'option for the poor' of Liberation Theology, yet it is not an explicit theological concern in Merton's thought. The point of contact is in that Merton, in denying the world, denies, not the sacramental goodness of creation (in which he rejoices) but its false values and idols. Feminism, in being world-affirming, both affirms bodiliness in the face of the negative, spiritualising tradition on the body in much of Western spirituality, and proposes a world-transforming agenda; as Adrienne Rich's oft-quoted words put it:

> My heart is moved by all I cannot save:
> so much has been destroyed
>
> I have to cast my lot with those
> who age after age, perversely,
>
> with no extraordinary power,
> reconstitute the world.[19]

Feminist Theology is built on a rock-like conviction that knowing God, loving God, cannot be separated from justice-making. So a sentence of Merton's such as 'Go into the desert, not to escape other men, but in order to find them in God'[20] is simply not relevant to those women who find themselves already in a desert of

[18] The book which resulted from the dialogue is Mary John Mananzan et al., eds, *Women Resisting Violence: a Spirituality for Life* (Maryknoll: Orbis, 1996).

[19] Adrienne Rich, 'Natural Resources' in *The Dream of a Common Language* (New York: W. W. Norton, 1978), p. 67.

[20] T. Merton, *Seeds of Contemplation* (London: Burns & Oates, 1949), p. 20.

exclusion, whose solitude is based on isolation and alienation. It is certainly not relevant to those women in drought-stricken areas of many Third World countries who go into the desert daily in search of water. Feminist Theology begins with this clear awareness of the *political context of solitude*, but nonetheless seeks the face of God in this experience.

It is in the search for the authentic self that there is an amazing congruence between Merton and feminist theological insights. I discern three aspects. The first is that Merton's life-long struggle against the illusory, false self – seen in all his writings from *Seeds of Contemplation* and *Conjectures of a Guilty Bystander*, to the later work influenced by Zen and Eastern mysticism[21] – is paralleled by Feminist Theology's search for an authentic self for women nurtured – and not suppressed – by Christian theology. In fact Merton's 'no-self' (a Buddhist concept) finds an echo in the feminist search for self on the basis of experiencing oneself as nothing, literally 'no-thing'.[22] Carol Christ, in her groundbreaking book on feminist quest, *Diving Deep and Surfacing*, explores the desperation of women as we come to realise that women's experience of being a self – in its enormous diversity of race and class – is not reflected in the dominant understanding of selfhood. Jean Baker Miller admitted that women frequently develop a sense of self which is so mediated through husband, father, children, brother, that the word 'self' is a misnomer.[23] So the 'no-thing' which is positive in Merton is negative in feminism: to be abused, despised, accounted as a non-person, this is what we have to resist in the name of the kingdom of peace and justice. But it is in the stripping away of the false self – the way of

---

[21] A helpful resource for Merton's theology of the self is Anne Carr, *A Search for Wisdom and Spirit: Thomas Merton's Theology of the Self* (Indiana: University of Notre Dame Press, 1988).

[22] See Carol Christ, *Diving Deep and Surfacing* (Boston: Beacon, 1980).

[23] See Jean Baker Miller, *Towards a New Psychology of Women* (Boston: Beacon, 1978), pp. 76–7: 'Women are encouraged to transform their drives into the service of another's drives; and the mediation is not directly with reality, but with and through the other person's purpose in that reality.' See also the discussion in M. Grey, *Redeeming the Dream*, op. cit., pp. 15–27.

kenoticism – that we find the congruence with Merton and, indeed, with the exhortation of Jesus. Feminist Theology has been active in pointing to the dangers of extolling the death of self which, it is claimed, is the gospel injunction to every disciple.[24] The Dutch feminist theologian Annelies van Heijst, in her book *Longing for the Fall,* showed how the experience of the death of self could have three different outcomes.[25] Either a person re-discovers a sense of self on the same basis – recovers confidence and pride, after, for example, depression, bereavement, failure; or he or she recovers self on a different basis, which could be according to the traditional model of the dominant self, achieving selfhood through controlling others; or it could be a selfhood attained on a totally different basis – the feminist self, achieved in solidarity, mutuality and relationship with others, in particular with the poor and oppressed – across a range of real life situations.

Secondly, Merton's views on the self in solitude find a reson-ance within feminist insights. He is careful to distinguish solitude (his early criticisms of the way we try to avoid solitude and fill up the day with noise and meaningless activities[26] certainly ring true!) from 'separation'. Whether he speaks of the inner or external self, the false or true self, the separate, individualist self or the authentic self, his sense of discovering connection with the human race while in solitude is exactly what is meant by the 'connected aloneness' of the feminist mystic,[27] or what I have

[24] See M. Grey, *Redeeming the Dream,* ibid.

[25] Annelies van Heijst, *Longing for the Fall* (Kampen: Kok Pharos, 1994).

[26] Merton, *Seeds of Contemplation* (London: Burns & Oates, 1949), p. 32: 'Interior solitude is impossible for them. They fear it. They do everything they can to escape it. . . . They are great promoters of useless work. They love to organize meetings and banquets and conferences and lectures. They print circulars, write letters, talk for hours on the telephone in order that they may gather together a hundred people in a large room where they will fill the air with smoke and make a great deal of noise and roar at one another and clap their hands and stagger home at last, patting one another on the back with the assurance that they have all done great things to spread the Kingdom of God.'

[27] See Margaret Miles, 'The Courage to be Alone – in and out of Marriage', in Mary E. Giles, ed., *The Feminist Mystic* (New York: Crossroad, 1985), pp. 84–102.

developed as 'epiphanies of connectedness', moments of divine grace and revelation.[28] As he says,

> The person must be rescued from the individual. The free son (!) of God must be saved from the conformist slave of fantasy, passion and convention. The creative and mysterious inner self must be delivered from the wasteful, hedonistic and destructive ego that seeks only to cover itself with disguises.[29]

The experience of being freed from a solitude which separates and the recovery of a passion for connectedness were, of course, revealed by his famous Louisville vision:

> In Louisville . . . in the center of the shopping district, I was suddenly overwhelmed with the realisation that I loved all those people, that they were mine and I theirs, that we could not be alien to one another even though we were total strangers. It was like waking from a dream of separateness, of spurious isolation in a special world, the world of renunciation and supposed holiness . . . I have the immense joy of being . . . a member of a race in which God Himself became incarnate . . . There is no way of telling people that they are walking round shining like the sun.[30]

It is striking that this moment of revelation – an epiphany of connection – is linked with Merton writing the prose-poem *Hagia Sophia*, with God entering creation as the feminine figure of Sophia/Wisdom, and seeing this incarnation of Sophia, in sophianic figures like Lara in *Dr Zhivago*.[31] Without entering into pontifications on Merton's relationships with women, about which so much has been written, what I think is important for my argument is my intuition that his thought would have developed from the abstractions of Sophia and the idealisation of

---

[28] See M. Grey, *The Wisdom of Fools?* (London: SPCK, 1993), pp. 60ff.

[29] From *New Seeds of Contemplation*. Cited by Shannon, *Thomas Merton's Dark Path*, op. cit., p. 156.

[30] Thomas Merton, *Conjectures of a Guilty Bystander* (London: Burns & Oates, 1965), pp. 156–7.

[31] See Anne Carr, op. cit., p. 71.

the feminine, into making concrete connections with the real lives and sufferings of women as women.

What I would like to develop now is the way that the insights of Merton's Louisville vision and a feminist spirituality based on 'epiphanies of connection' offer a way forward from the tension between 'escape the world or change the world', fruitful for the project of the recovery of community. This is a spirituality which also addresses my other two points – the search for God which respects and fosters a true sense of dependence, and the hope of life in all its fullness. Both of these lie at the heart of authentic ecclesial community.

Epiphanies of connection: Merton's link with a feminist spirituality

Merton's call to get rid of the false and illusory self is linked with the distinction made today between the 'disengaged self', constantly called to great ethical projects (we could also make the connections today with the travelling business executive, the absent father, or mother!), and the 'relational self' (or even the 'ecological self'), investing total identity in relationships – which could be either positive or destructive. This ambiguity is also found in my second point, which is the contemplative search for complete dependence on (abandonment to?) God. Clearly, for the contemplative or mystic total abandonment to God's love is the ideal. Yet for women, notions of dependence mean demeaning situations of economic poverty or emotional dependence which can cripple the development of the autonomous self. Sarah Coakley also questions the link between the nature of abandonment language and its sexual innuendoes:

> What feminist theology is fundamentally about, in my opinion, is an unresolved dilemma, a fundamental aporia in the Christian tradition, about the relationship between sexual desire on the one hand and desire for God on the other.[32]

---

[32] Sarah Coakely, op. cit., Lecture 1, p. 17.

Merton was unaware of the effects on women of Christian (and other faiths') insistence on obedience and submission of will as the path to sanctity. It is now very clear that the complex structure of kyriarchy can function to block all development of freely chosen self-giving for women. Merton was also unaware of the connotations for women of words like 'innocence' and 'purity', where sexual innocence has been made a bargaining tool for marriages and a means of imprisonment for young girls in order to achieve a lucrative match. Nor can the achievement of 'life in all its fullness' even be realistically hoped for, without understanding the political and social contexts for words to which we attach theological meaning.

In order to discover a way out of the impasse I explore here the ideas of Etty Hillesum, a young Jewish woman who died in Auschwitz, particularly her notion of 'soulscape', together with my own notion of the connected and ecological self.[33] Etty Hillesum lived and worked in Amsterdam at the time of the German occupation, so the narrowing opportunities for joyous living form the background to her journal. Deportations and starvation are its backcloth, as are her own relationship with an extraordinary man, Julius Spier, a chiropractor, and at the same time her growing relationship with God. It was a scenario that Merton would have understood. Her idea of soulscape links interior growth with outward circumstances, in a way that bridges some of the duality we are struggling with. Here Etty Hillesum describes a train journey:

> The train to Deventer. The open skies, peaceful and also a little sad. I look out of the window and it is as if I were riding through the landscapes of my own soul. Soul-landscape. I feel like that often: that the outer landscape is the reflection of the inner. Thursday afternoon along the River Ijssel. A radiant, sweeping, bright, landscape. (p. 80)

Creating a soulscape is not about writing mystical poetry to encapsulate all experience. It is more about connecting the fragmented

---

[33] Etty Hillesum, *An Interrupted Life: The Diaries of Etty Hillesum 1941–3* (Washington Square Press, 1981).

elements of the physical, material, psychological and emotional elements of all of our lives, with an intensity and a desire for wholeness – the root meaning of salvation. It means a thoroughly ecological view of self. Every environmental detail – landscape, weather, diet, health possibilities, air pollution – contributes to the landscape of the self, to the possibilities of this soulscape. It requires patient awareness and a kind of connecting perception. Merton might call it a 'sacramental perception'. Etty Hillesum is full of such details as 'gas fire, yellow and red tulips, an unexpected piece of chocolate . . . three fircones,' (p. 81) and a sense of joy emanates which reminds me of the tenderness with which the painter Chagall paints ordinary things (Merton loved Chagall's 'angelic innocence'). Soul-landscape is about relating to these elements of ordinariness with tenderness, reverence and a sense of gratefulness, integrating them all into a process of self-becoming. Etty Hillesum describes the extraordinary transformation that overcame her. This passage is in the context of her relationship with Julius Spier – the greatest influence in her life (it is written within the context of scarcity of food):

> We managed with great difficulty to get three lemons from a barrow . . . But we were determined to have some cake and whipped cream. And then we roamed the streets again . . . and now it's nearly 8.30. The last evening of a year that has been the most fruitful, and yes, the happiest of all. And if I had to put in a nutshell what this year has meant . . . then I would say: greater awareness and hence easier access to my inner sources. (p. 81)

I recognise here Merton's great appreciation of food and companionship. But the extra element here is that this enjoyment is linked with a relationship with God. From being 'the girl who couldn't kneel, couldn't pray' – her laughing description of herself – Etty Hillesum became propelled by a sense of cosmic awareness, being part of a greater whole, forced on to her knees in response. And this deepened until, towards the end, she wanted to be nothing but prayer. As the external scene became increasingly more fragmented, with the beginnings of the deportations to the camps (Etty Hillesum went voluntarily with one of the first groups to the labour camps), this sense of inner strength grew. She described the ruin of the jasmine outside her house. But the flourishing of the jasmine within brought an increased sense of responsibility to God for all the people and the evil of their actions:

> And it spreads its scent around the House in which you dwell, O God. You see, I can look after you, I bring not only my tears, and my forebodings on this stormy, grey, Sunday morning, I even bring you scented jasmine. I shall try to make You at home always, even should I be locked in a narrow cell, and a cloud should drift past my small barred window, then I shall bring you that cloud, O God, while there is still strength in me to do so. (p. 188)

Can this sense of taking responsibility for God, recognising the vulnerability of God, lift us from the difficulty of how to nurture a real dependence on God while crushed with debilitating deprivations? When starving, fearful, isolated, does the intuition that God, too, is vulnerable and can suffer from our false notions of dependency, bring any sense of empowerment? Etty Hillesum blazes a trail by affirming the need to strip away crippling notions of dependency and obedience through affirming life in its fullness, despite the horrors of the present. Chung Hyun Kyung, the Korean liberation theologian, at the dialogue in Costa Rica mentioned earlier, told the poignant story of the Korean 'comfort woman' Soo Bock who, in the midst of her degrading and shocking treatment by the Japanese soldiers, chose not death but life. She chose to eat, did whatever the soldiers told her, because she had decided to survive – unlike many of her companions. She did survive, and today, at 74 years, she is a great strength for reconciliation. What gave her strength to survive, asked Hyun Kyung. The affirmation of life in all its fullness? The complete loss of self (Soo Bock is a Buddhist) – but a finding of the *connected self* because of this?

   This awakening to the connected self, to the ecological self, is accompanied by the awareness of being part of a larger, interconnected whole. Yet the sense of smallness within this – what Buddhists call the 'jewelled net of the Lord Indra', in which all interconnecting nodes reflect each other yet retain their own identity – does not diminish the sense of responsibility for the specific context. I mean responsibility in its primary sense of 'being responsive to' as well as responsible for. Etty's 'responsiveness to' brought a vocation of responding to the suffering of the people in the camps, of refusing (like Soo Bock) to give way to hatred of the enemy, of accommodating something of that terrible suffering, of anticipating the whole burden of sorrow. Secondly, in the deepening awareness comes realisation of the *broken connections*, the polluted sky, earth, water, the poisoned lakes, the dying species, the lost connections with the animal world, the missing language of relation, the inherited wounds of our families, our institutions, structures in the work-place, the inadequacy of the patterns of caring we received. Connection is reconnecting . . . Connection is rebuilding fragmented selves in a fragmented world. As Adrienne Rich wrote,

> Freedom. It isn't once, to walk out
> under the Milky Way, feeling the rivers
> of light, the fields of dark –
> freedom is daily, prose-bound, routine
> remembering. Putting together inch by inch
> the starry worlds. From all the lost collections.[34]

Merton spoke of being married to the silence of the forest:

> One might say I had decided to marry the silence of the forest. The sweet dark warmth of the world will have to be my wife. Out of the heart of that dark warmth comes the secret that is heard only in silence.[35]

What he speaks of as 'the secret that is heard only in silence' becomes in a spirituality of epiphanies of connectedness a way of healing fragmentation and brokenness. It is putting together the fragmented pieces of our broken selves; it is creating a soulscape by giving our emotions time and space, respecting bodily rhythms; it is 're-membering' in the sense of joining together the fragments

[34] Adrienne Rich, 'For Memory' in *A Wild Patience has Taken me thus Far* (New York: W. W. Norton, 1981), p. 22

[35] 'Day of a Stranger' in *A Thomas Merton Reader*, ed. Thomas P. McDonnell (New York: Harcourt, Brace & World, 1962), p. 434.

into a different whole, even through reaching backwards into the past. Adrienne Rich, in another haunting passage in 'The Spirit of Place,' combines the connecting of self with environment, as well as with re-membering our past foremothers:

> The world as it is: not as her users boast
> damaged beyond reclamation by their using
> Ourselves as we are   in these painful motions
>
> of staying cognizant: some part of us always
> out beyond ourselves
> knowing   knowing   knowing . . .
> On a pure night   on a night when pollution
>
> seems absurdity when the undamaged planet seems to turn
> like a bowl of crystal in black ether
> they are the piece of us that lies out there
> knowing   knowing   knowing.[36]

A spirituality of connectedness can be encapsulated in the theme of the prophetic *heart*. I have chosen in this chapter to focus on soulscape because of integrating interiority with external political and social circumstances into a contemplative faith responsive, in freedom, to the vulnerability of God. God's true dwelling is in the depths of the human person. Yet Christian spirituality refers more often to the *heart* as integrating centre. 'Cor ad Cor loquitur', as Newman said – and we are spoken to from the depths. But Etty Hillesum gives another depth to the indwelling of God. Again it is rooted in God's vulnerability:

> Alas, there doesn't seem very much You yourself can do about our circumstances, our lives . . . you cannot help us but we must help you to defend Your dwelling place inside us to the last. . . . (p. 187)

> Sometimes they [people] seem to me like houses with open doors. I walk in and roam through passages and rooms, and every house is furnished a little differently and yet they are all of them the same, and every one must be turned into a dwelling dedicated to

---

[36] Adrienne Rich, 'The Spirit of Place' in *A Wild Patience has Taken me thus Far*, op. cit., p. 45.

you, O God. And I promise you, yes, I promise that I shall try to find a dwelling and refuge for you in as many houses as possible. There are so many empty houses, and I shall prepare them all for you, the most honoured Lodger. Please forgive this poor metaphor. (p. 215)

The human heart, God's dwelling, and the responsibility to make God welcome in all the empty houses – is it here that we find the reconciliation of the tension between solitude and community with which this chapter began? Is it here that we solve the dichotomy 'escape the world or change the world'? We may, as Merton said, 'be exiles at the far end of solitude living as listeners, with hearts attending to the skies we cannot understand',[37] but through epiphanies of connection, freely given – at Louisville or elsewhere, we are offered glimpses of the eros or yearning of God as indwelling presence in all of us. This is uncrushable hope in our fragmented world.

Conclusion

By bringing Merton into dialogue with some of the insights of Feminist Theology I have tried to show that contemplation, far from being an escape from the responsibilities of the world, through the metaphor of connectedness can be reimagined as a deeper engagement with it, specifically as engaging with the fragmentation of culture which threatens to engulf us. I need now to show how becoming a self, connected yet contemplative, emerges from the very core of Christian community. But to do this I must first explore how the idea of Church is integrally linked with a theology of relation, where self-in-community, empowered by a relational God, engages in the process of gathering the fragments of a broken world. And this will be the focus of chapter 2.

[37] Thomas Merton, *The Climate of Monastic Prayer* (Spencer, MA: Cistercian Publications, 1969).

2

'In the beginning
is the relation'

The roots and wings of a Relational Theology

Introduction

I began with the age–old Christian tension between fleeing the world or changing the world, and tried to show that it was a false dilemma. My next task is to try to show that the only hope of overcoming competitive individualism with all its attendant features is through counter-cultural communities which live by a different vision and ethic. Whereas in chapter 3 I will argue for a contemplative way of life as liberation from the 'Dark Night of the Church', here I explore a more basic level of the dilemma. The argument will be that:

- the basic structure of the human person is relational, so that human becoming can only be achieved in community; yet this relational notion of personhood is counter-cultural to competitive individualism;

- this is the fundamental insight of Christian discipleship and community, embodied in the praxis and ministry of Jesus of Nazareth;

- this is so because God's very self is relational; God is the power to make right relation; God even created the world out of a yearning for relation. But if this is true, then God is vulnerable to our response; and redemption is dependent on our being empowered by a vulnerable God (this was the insight of Etty Hillesum, already cited in the previous chapter).

23

To be a person is to live from the yeast of connectedness or from a matrix of connections

I begin with a very homely and personal image of my grandmother. When I was a child – the eldest of seven children – I knew what the web of relations in an extended family meant. We lived in the North-East of England, in a street with six houses. We lived in No. 2, a great-aunt in No. 4, and my grandmother and two other aunts in No. 6. As children, we were aware that, in a certain sense, 'wisdom dwelt in No. 6', for our mother would frequently send us to ask our grandmother if it was a good day for hanging the washing out to dry, or a question about cooking. We had the security of knowing that if things got a bit too hot for us in our own house, we were welcome in No. 6, where some aunt would be sure to have baked chocolate cake or apple pie![1] My grandmother as a carpet-maker is the reason for citing this childhood experience. She was a war widow who had been left with eight children and a pension of 26 shillings a week. What gave her great authority in the eyes of us children were the times when the great carpet-frame was set up in her kitchen. For days on end she would work on a carpet for whoever needed it, and the whole family would come in and out, supplying her with materials – literally, pieces of coats, skirts and cloaks; a veritable kaleidoscope of our interconnected lives was woven into each carpet. And, of course, far more than simply the materials. She, with her history of foremothers and fathers surviving the great Irish famine of 1845, of being both father and mother to my mother and all her siblings; she, vulnerable to all the tragic aftermath of two wars, is a real flesh and blood icon of relational strength. Through this simple story I recognise the matrix of connections which – partly – makes me what I am. And each one of us exists from these matrices, as we interconnect with each others' histories, memories, family trees, shared values and hopes.

At this time I remember my grandmother, who knew such a harsh beginning of the century with the death of her husband, and

[1] My sister Barbara has even written an (unpublished) article, 'Heaven and No. 6'.

24

a life of poverty right through it (although then I never knew it), because at the end of the same century we face the shattered fragments of society and have lost the security that my grandmother never questioned. And, as theologians, we have to ask what responsibility our theological beliefs should take, now that the great rationalist project of the Enlightenment has come adrift so badly.

In chapter 1 I cited only the fact of individualism and consumerism as contributory causes to the violence in our society. I did not cite the worsening spirals of poverty in the poor southern hemisphere, the South which is directly vulnerable to northern economics and politics. Yet, as is well known, in the last 25 years, and since the publication of warning documents like *The Limits to Growth*,[2] the South–North gap has widened. A recent quotation from the *Guardian* put it starkly and succinctly:

> The Rich, they say, will always be with us. But never in the history of the world have they been present in such quantities and in such flamboyant contrast with the poor as now. The year's most halting statistic has come in the UN's new Human Development Report. Take it in slowly: the total wealth of the world's 358 billionaires equals the combined incomes of the poorest 45 per cent of the world's population – 2.3 billion people.[3]

Small wonder that, in a dialogue with me, the Czech theologian Jana Opocenska, facing the loss of vision which Central Europe has experienced since the fall of Communism, wrote: 'We have to recognize that civilisation has reached its lowest point.'[4]

---

[2] Dennis Meadows et al., *The Limits to Growth* (Washington DC: Potomac Associates, 1972). Another resource which made an impact in the same year was Barbara Ward and René Dubos, *Only One Earth: the Care and Maintenance of a Small Planet* (Harmondsworth: Penguin, 1972). A much more recent work, showing how these earlier warnings have been ignored, and how poverty and environmental problems are increasing, is Paul Harrison, *Inside the Third World* (London: I. B. Tauris & Co., 1992).

[3] Victor Keegan, 'Highway Robbery by the Super-Rich', *Guardian*, 22 July 1996, p. 23.

[4] Mary Grey and Jana Opocenska, 'East meets West: a Dialogue', in *Jahrbuch of the European Society of Women in Theological Research*, 1 (August 1994), pp. 9–19.

So, speaking of a culture in fragments refers not only to our own society, but to fragmentation at a global level. It means challenging the roots of our theology; my fear is that the way we image God and the whole mystery of salvation/redemption, sin and grace, continues to underpin the cruel abuse of power and the continual ability of the rich and powerful to claim God on their side. Is it possible that our theological categories are linked with the way compassion – since Nietzsche's attack – is considered an emotion for the weak? Is it possible that our dualistic thought-patterns produce the ability – shared by all the Christian Churches[5] – to live with a presumed inevitability of poverty, particularly the structural causes of poverty, through blaming the individual for not making it in life? What I suggest is that the relational model underpinning the traditional theistic God of power and might is a severely damaged one, and continues to inspire *disordered relations* – on personal, interpersonal and structural levels. So to discover the God of right relation means both discovering, as Etty Hillesum showed us, the vulnerable, not the omnipotent, God, and *being empowered by the paradoxical strength of her vulnerability*.

To discover what this means for Christian communities seeking for a lifestyle witness of justice and truth, I shall first explore the roots of Relational Theology. Secondly, I shall take this as a basis for ethics. And thirdly, I shall show how Relational Theology can take wings, opening up new orientations for theology itself.

Roots

The question of starting point is crucial. It is not a question of testing one theoretic framework against another – scholastic, reformed, transcendental, existential, neo-Thomist, Barthian, and so on. It is

---

[5] See the Report of Christian Aid, *The Gospel, The Poor and the Churches* (Christian Aid, 1992). The outcome of this research suggested that the attitudes to poverty from a range of sixteen Church denominations studied, varied little. When reacting to poverty in this country, many felt that the blame lay with the individual him or herself. If some can make the effort, why not all? But when dealing with poverty on a global scale, distancing mechanisms came into play, as the problems were felt to be too vast for an effective response.

partly because of the failure of these models to provide the transformative leaven of society that culture needs a new foundation
and a fresh start. I suggest that we start with the two nodal points
for a liberation theology – *praxis* and *experience* – flawed though
these may seem. The focus on praxis (that is, the spiralling
process of action/reflection) means that I want to bring theology
– often sidelined as theoretic reflection – to bear on what
actually changes lives and communities. The hope is that *Relational*
Theology will inspire a different sort of praxis and that theologising
will once more be restored as the activity of the whole community-
in-relationship. Secondly, the focus on experience also locates
theology as the activity whereby God is seen to touch peoples' lives
as inspirational centre. Relational faith means experiencing and
believing in God as holding our relational nexuses together: God
is tasted as the yeast which gives them savour and transformative
potential. As Catherine Keller wrote: 'We meet God as the molten
core of heart's desire, ever energising our courage and our quest.'[6]

But, as is well known, experience is a suspect word, and
whose experience is to be privileged is the question. When I first
began theology in the 1960s, I was consumed with the idea that
theology should impinge on and transform ordinary experience.[7]
But I did not then understand that the theology I learnt (this was
at the University of Louvain, Belgium) and the sources from which

---

[6] Catherine Keller, *From a Broken Web* (Boston: Beacon, 1986), p. 215. The
idea of tasting and savouring God is suggested by Edwina Gately's book, *A Rich,
Warm, Moist, Salty God* (Trabuco Canyon CA: Source Books, 1993).

[7] I was very influenced by the writings of Rosemary Haughton, for example,
The Knife-Edge of Experience (London: Darton, Longman & Todd, 1972). It was
she who taught me to look for God's presence and action through a range of life
experiences – and to understand literature as a rich resource for this. She outlines
two sorts of theology, the prophetic and the reflective, both of which need to
draw on authentic experience. I quote the conclusion (p. 168): 'for if there is one
lesson which emerges from the varieties and forms of Christian experience it is
that a truthful theology requires a truthful expression of experience . . . But the
spiritual integrity and sensitivity required of the Christian is more far-reaching
than that of the poet, because it has to prepare him not only to face experience
fully, but to take decisions on the basis of that experience, as he interprets it in
the light of the Gospel. And these decisions not only commit the individual, but

I eagerly drank did not touch upon the experience of ordinary people, and it certainly did not – at that point[8] – include the experience of women. The theology of experience has often meant little more than, for example, decorating dry theological arguments with a few poems, a few anecdotes, and focusing on the theology of marriage and sexuality as supposedly closer to experience. Putting cream on the dry theological tart, one might say.

It was not until much later – well after those heady first days of Liberation Theology – that I discovered ideas like 'the underside of history' and read the works of the philosopher/historian, the late Michel Foucault, with his call for the 'insurrection of the subjugated knowledges'.[9] Here Foucault, in examining resistance to dominant forms of power and knowledge identified a strain which opposed an established form of discourse. These 'subjugated knowledges' refer to a whole group of knowledges pointing to the specific history of subjugation, conflict and domination which have been lost or deliberately erased by the discourse of those holding power.[10] I realised instantly that the wisdom of my grandmother had a place in this scheme. Not only was the experience of women, of poor women, of groups robbed of their land like the North American Indians, of those considered not to be fully human (like the mentally-handicapped), of those whose sexual orientation placed them at the bottom of the heap, now worthy of consideration; but, from a theological

---

the sum and the tendency of them commits the whole people, truthfully or not. *Theology has to be the result of the whole Church reflecting on its experience, and the theology will be true to the Spirit of Christ when, and only when, it is the poetry of a whole people'* (my italics). This is a rich insight, but one which, in 1972, was not yet gender-specific.

[8] Since 1993 there has been a Professor of Womens' Studies Theology at the University of Louvain/Leuven. Its present holder is Professor Dr Hedwig Meyer Wilmes, my colleague from *Feminisme en Christendom* at the University of Nijmegen, The Netherlands.

[9] Michel Foucault, *Power/Knowledge: Selected Interviews and Other Writings*, 1972–7, tr. C. Gordon, L. Marshall, J. Mepham and K. Soper (New York and London: Pantheon, 1980), p. 81.

[10] I have discussed this in *Redeeming the Dream*, op. cit., pp. 8–9.

perspective (and this is departing from Foucault), these know-ledges were to be privileged.[11] The justification, for ourselves as theologians, for prioritising the life experience, the wisdom and the hidden, suppressed and subjugated knowledges of poor people, is that Jesus identified these as the priority for the Kingdom of God:

> The blind receive their sight and the lame walk, lepers are cleansed and the deaf hear, and the dead are raised up, and the poor have the good news preached to them. (Mt 11.5)

This is a far cry from the self-indulgent interpretation of experience often encountered in the West through the demands of the 'me-generation'; this issues from the 'finding myself' form of spiritu-ality, what I call 'salvation-in-the-sauna'. In chapter 1 I cited the hermeneutical priority of 'If it's good for poor women, it's good for all', from the Costa Rica dialogue; what this points to is that the interweaving of gospel priorities and the experience and praxis of the underside of history has to be the inspiration for Christian community.[12]

It is our inspiration for a second reason. Experience and praxis as key organising concepts are embedded in complex relational contexts. It is the fundamental energy of life as relational which gives them this place of privilege. The inspirations for this idea flow together from many sources which include the philosophy of Martin Buber and his famous *I and Thou*, from new cosmology, systems theory and Process Theology; these can all be con-sidered as roots or ingredients of Relational Theology. They all coalesce as Feminist Theology gathers them into the formation of a relational theology, where the key concepts are mutuality,

---

[11] I am very aware that the categories of who exactly are to be privileged are shifting ones, as ever-new groups enter our consciousness and become ethical priorities.

[12] Experience is also problematic for another reason. What is the *content* of the experience which is to be privileged? Is the mere fact of being excluded and oppressed, considered as an inferior human subject, the factor to be privileged? Clearly we need careful contextual analysis as to how the authority of the inclu-sion of 'women's experience' is to influence and transform the understanding of social realities.

reciprocity, interdependence, a passion for right relation, and the just interconnectedness of all things. But the fundamental *theological* insight is of a Creator God who creates out of a yearning for relation, the God whose fundamental creative energy is not primarily the *speaking word* but the *relation from which it is bodied forth:*

> For in the beginning is the relation, and in the relation is the power which creates the world, through us and with us and by us, you and I, you and we, and none of us alone.[13]

What I understand to be happening here is that it is on the *relational context*, where communication happens, that stress is laid.[14] Not only that, but the nature of the relational context is crucial. Is it oppressive? Is it one which hears into speech the silenced voices? Buber restored mutuality to the word, but we cannot distinguish God's passion for relation from God's passion for justice: the two are inseparable. As Carter Heyward put it powerfully:

> With you I begin to realise that the sun can rise again, the rivers can flow again, the fires can burn again. With you I begin to see that the hungry can eat again, the children can play again, the women can rage and stand again. It is not a matter of what ought to be. It is a power that drives to justice and makes it. Makes the sun blaze, the rivers roar, the fires rage. And the revolution is won again. And you and I are pushed by a power both terrifying and comforting. And to say 'I love you' means 'Let the revolution begin!'[15]

In a world where power means military might, spawning an ethic of domination/submission (in other words, kyriarchy, the rule of the Lord), where cultures of violence are the norm (a violence which comprehends areas of economic, political and ecological violence as well as military), relational power and the dynamics of mutual

---

[13] Carter Heyward, *The Redemption of God: a Theology of Mutual Relation* (Washington: University of America Press, 1980), p. 172. She is building on the insights of Martin Buber.

[14] The English theologian Nicholas Lash (see *Easter in Ordinarie* [London: SCM, 1988]) has asked whether Buber really meant to remove the priority of the word; he concludes that he is trying to restore mutuality to its expression.

[15] Heyward, op. cit., p. 162.

empowerment are fragile. They are unpredictable in the sense of not being guaranteed by structures or laws. Like the experience of 'Thou-ness' of which Martin Buber spoke so movingly, relational power can arise spontaneously.[16] But this – the way God works in the world – follows the dynamics of grace in being both invitation and response. Catherine Keller writes sadly that relational power is not likely to win:

> The lines of relational power, more like fibers in a web than railroad tracks to the horizon, intersect and energize communities of support and struggle already. This latter strategy does not await a Messiah astride his white horse, leading hoards of final angels. Rather, it will nurture the delicate and nonetheless messianic power of awakened relations.[17]

Building blocks of Relational Theology

I will now try to spell this out in building blocks – or threads in the cosmic weave of relatedness, recalling the image with which I began, of my grandmother's carpet making. The stronger I can make the case for authentic relational personhood, the stronger the argument for *ecclesia* as the home for human flourishing – human, but always in connection with the non-human creation.

First, Process Theology in its own dynamics presents a theology that is deeply relational, in which 'to be actual is to be in process'[18] and in movement: 'in the seeking is the finding'. Relating is the only way of moving forward. It is also the creative interaction between God and humanity, in which every human being's experience – every unit of experience – is taken up into God and then re-offered as the possibility for new becoming.[19] Thus the way is open for us to understand that human activity has an effect

[16] Martin Buber, *I and Thou* (Edinburgh: T. & T. Clark, 1958, 2nd edn.).

[17] Catherine Keller, 'Power Lines' in *Theology Today* 5(2) (July 1995), p. 203.

[18] John Cobb Jr and David Griffin, *Process Theology – an Introductory Exposition* (Philadelphia: Westminster, 1976), p. 14.

[19] See M. Grey, Weaving New Visions: the Promise of Christian Feminist Process Thought for Christian Theology, Inaugural Lecture, University of Nijmegen, 1989; Marjorie Suchocki, *God, Christ, Church* (New York: Crossroad, 1988); M. Grey, *Redeeming the Dream*, op. cit., pp. 34–7.

on the being of God. This is one of the dimensions of divine vulnerability. As the closing pages of Whitehead's *Process and Reality* put it, 'God is the fellow-sufferer who understands'.[20] The relationship between God and the world is not a controlling one: this is not the omnipotent, impassible, unchangeable God of classical theism. As Whitehead put it:

> [God] does not create the world, he saves it; or, more accurately, he is the poet of the world, with tender patience leading it by his own vision of truth, beauty, goodness.[21]

Secondly, the way God interacts with humanity and all the processes of creation respects the two poles – the autonomy of the organism and its relational pole. Many physicists and cosmologists are now speaking of both the *integrative* and *assertive poles* of even minute organisms. The assertive pole is what preserves the distinctiveness and independence of the organism, especially when it is under threat. The relational, interacting pole is what is crucial for development and change. Whitehead speaks of the process of change and ongoing development as both adventure and risk. There is now even a tendency to accept that many parts of the universe may be interconnected in an immediate way, a claim previously made only by mystics and non-scientific people. It is quite extraordinary to absorb the new climate of relations and the new developing discourse between science and religion. We have moved far away from the 'God of the gaps' pseudo-discourse of the beginning of this century. One physicist, Paul Davies, describes the theory of super-symmetry according to which the basic units of the universe are not particles but 'wiggling motions of strings, like notes on a piano wire'[22] – a much more relational notion than 'self-sufficient atoms'. (It can be no accident that 'atomistic individualism' is frequently the phrase used to describe the currently-prevailing view of the human person.)

---

[20] A. N. Whitehead, *Process and Reality* (Cambridge: Macmillan Educational, 1929; corrected edn., New York: The Free Press, 1978), p. 472.

[21] Ibid., pp. 525–6.

[22] Quoted by Walter Schwarz, *Guardian*, 6 April 1987.

But the question for theologians is whether it is legitimate to make the jump from the structure of minute organisms to the complex structure of the human person, a move I want to make tentatively – even if I can only do it by analogy or metaphorically. Just as micro-organisms need both autonomous and integrative axes, it is reasonable to assume this is so both for the human person-in-relationship and for the dynamics of community. If this can be established – that harmonious interaction of every organism is the basic stuff of cosmic energy – there is a basis for challenging the relational nexus (or complexity of relational networks by which we live) according to whether both relational and autonomous poles of the human personality-in-relationship are being respected, and whether this nexus is a just one.

I will explore this in two ways. How does it work on the plane of economics? Society and its institutions – the World Bank, the Stock Exchange, Structural Adjustment Programmes – in their deliberations consider only the autonomous pole, arguing for what is financially profitable for their particular company and organisation. The relational pole is frequently ignored – or, rather, it is an unjust relational structure which tramples on the needs of the poorer countries.

The model can also be seen from the perspective of developmental psychology. There is a gender difference in the socialisation of young children: from an early age little girls are socialised into developing the relational axis of their personalities, so that they grow up to understand themselves as relational beings – as mothers of, daughters of, wives of, servants of . . . But the autonomous pole is lost sight of, so that the 'ego-integrity' which is achieved (to use the developmental psychologist Eric Erickson's term) has weak boundaries, scarcely deserving the name of ego.[23] The skills of empathic connection mean that it is hard for many women to be fully aware of where they stop and the other starts.[24] Hence the

---

[23] See Eric Erikson, *Childhood and Society* (New York: W. W. Norton, 1963).
[24] See Jean Baker-Miller, *Towards a New Psychology of Women*, cited in chapter 1; Carol Gilligan, *In a Different Voice?* (Harvard University Press, 1982); M. Grey, *Redeeming the Dream*, op. cit., chapter 2; Nancy Chodorow, *Gender and the Reproduction of Mothering* (University of California Press, 1978).

crucial importance of the relational nexus – of both micro and macro entities – respecting both the poles of independence and mutuality, always embodied in just structures.

The third factor builds on this fundamental interrelating energy. As I intimated, new accounts of cosmology are expressing this same interconnectedness as being the fundamental energy of creation. But the amazing thing is that this need not be understood reductionistically, as atoms interlocking to form larger units; the energy involved in the process can actually be characterised as a tenderness, as caring. This seems rather extraordinary! Yet the cosmologist Brian Swimme not only speaks of interconnectedness as raw cosmic energy, but adds that the nature of this is the allure, the attraction, between organisms or, in human terms, love:

> The great mystery is that we are interested in anything whatsoever. Think of your friends, how you met them, how interesting they appeared to you. Why should anyone in the whole world interest us at all? Why don't we experience everyone as utter, unendurable bores? Why isn't the cosmos made that way? Why don't we suffer intolerable boredom with every person, forest, symphony, and seashore in existence? The great surprise is the discovery that something or someone is interesting. Love begins there. Love begins when we discover interest. To be interested is to fall in love. To become fascinated is to step into a wild love affair on any level of life.[25]

This sense – love as the attraction, the relational energy which evokes and sustains the universe in both being and becoming is expressed in a variety of ways and most characteristically by the attitude of caring

This is my fourth point. It is the basic attitude of caring and attentiveness to all processes of creation which should be a prerequisite for all scientists. Thus the biologist Barbara McClintock has spoken of the necessity of the scientist to develop a 'feeling for the organism'.[26] On a mythological level, Heidegger's parable

[25] Brian Swimme, *The Universe is a Green Dragon* (Santa Fe: Bear & Co., 1984), p. 47.

[26] Barbara McClintock, as cited in Evelyn Fox Keller, *Reflections on Gender and Science* (Yale University Press, 1990), p. 165.

of Care, based on a old Roman legend, is expressing a similar point.[27] This tells of a dispute among the gods as to who should have responsibility for mortals. It is resolved by telling Care that as long as there is life, she is in control. So basic to human thriving is the quality of care which an infant experiences.[28]

Thus the ancient parable of Care expresses mythologically what is meant theologically by God's creative and redeeming love for the world (this was what Brian Swimme tried to express as the mysterious and surprising attraction between organisms). In Relational Theology this means God is a presence-in-power, actively sustaining healing patterns of relation, deepening the power of connectedness between humanity and all living things, calling us out of alienated patterns of relating. But it is not an exchanging of the transcendent for the immanent God. Rather, it is a re-imagining of both concepts. God is the molten core of our heart's desire, as Catherine Keller said (and you may recall the words of Augustine, 'God is deeper to me than my most intimate self'), but God is also the 'power of crossing over'. Literally this is Latin 'transcendere', the attraction, the love between things (Brian Swimme), the energy of making the connections in my own terminology. But the precondition for making ever-deepening connections is that relational power is vulnerable. And God as the pulsating heart of relating is paradoxically both vulnerable to our response and yet, at the same time, empowering us out of this very vulnerability. And the thread which draws this together for Christianity is the cross event; nowhere does God appear as more vulnerable and abandoned than on the cross, yet from no other event does Christian faith derive more empowerment. So the point of urgency for communities of faith is the pattern and structure of caring which is set in motion. The danger

[27] See M. Heidegger, *Being and Time* (Oxford: Blackwell, 1962), p. 242; the fable is actually no. 220 of the fables of Hyginus, and the text is from F. Buchler, *Rheinisches Museum* 41 (1886), p. 5.

[28] It is a well-known precondition for infant 'thriving' – a technical term – that caring involves more than food and warmth: it means affection, symbiotic bonding with the primary carer and a sense of belonging. See John Bowlby, *Child Care and the Growth of Love* (Harmondsworth: Penguin, 2nd edn., 1965).

is cooption by damaged societal patterns of caring, by line-management language, by patronising disempowerment, by a sentimentalising seasonal caring which fails to challenge the structures.

So, what kind of ethical paradigm is offered by Relational Theology in the teeth of worsening South–North connections, in a fragmenting culture? What hope for gathering the fragments?

The ethics of the Beloved Community

The question becomes: could re-imaging God as the vulnerable source of relational power, and seeing the whole Christ-event as embodiment and incarnation of relational power in action, actually make a difference to the way we behave? Could it work, in other words, as a basis for the ethics of the 'Beloved Community'?

The starting point has to be recognition of the way in which our basic patterns of knowing, perceiving and feeling are already damaged by the kyriarchal patterns of the ethics of domination, the structures of cultural and racial superiority, the language of binary oppositions, and the way all these come together in absolutising the 'individualistic I'. This 'enclosed I' which seeks 'mastery'without counting the cost cannot comprehend the language of relation. Full mutuality will never even be glimpsed by this 'enclosed I' of modernity, this narcissist who, as Catherine Keller says, 'never encounters the objectivity, the acute difference of the other, but uses the other for self-gratification'.[29]

So the second step is the deliberate moving out of the living patterns of the 'individualistic I' within an imperative of 'maximising connectedness'. The recovery of the relational, or connected, or even the 'ecological' self[30] is event, process and task. As I argued in chapter 1, if it is the false egoistic self which is lost,[31]

---

[29] Catherine Keller, *From a Broken Web*, op. cit., p. 192.

[30] See Freya Matthews, *The Ecological Self* (London: Routledge, 1991).

[31] There are many parallels here with the way Buddhism thinks of the self and the ego as illusion.

My heart recoils within me,
   my compassion grows warm and tender.
I will not execute my fierce anger,
   I will not again destroy Ephraim;
For I am God and not man,
   The Holy One in your midst,
   And I will not come to destroy. (11.8–9)

e sense of a God acting according to different ethical priori-
strong. The ability to see, to envision possibilities of dealing
iolence other than strikes either of revenge or pre-emption,
ine. The autobiography of Nelson Mandela has a moving
nt of the early days of the ANC, when non-violent action was
thos of the movement, even amidst the poverty and violent
ression of the apartheid government (Gandhi's son was then
of the leadership). Even when the exigency of the times led to
being changed to armed struggle, Mandela never succumbed
killing as the total answer. Now, in freedom, he has sought to
ild into the new constitution an alternative to vengeance. Truly
ving wings to freedom.

   This, the power of envisioning alternatives, the power to see, is
hat is meant by being empowered by a vulnerable God. It means
e-imaging vulnerability, not as weakness, but as the power of being
present to, of suffering-with, of encouraging, of facing the truth,
of respecting the fragility of shared humanness. Cutting off the
water supply, burning the crops, deliberately exploits our human
vulnerability. Abusing small children, impoverishing mothers, hits
the most vulnerable sections of humanity. Burning the forests
attacks the vulnerability of nature, which has no voice. For in the
vitality of the trees are both the roots and wings of human flourishing: as John Chrysostom's Good Friday Homily put it,

> The Tree is my eternal salvation. It is my nourishment and my
> banquet. Amidst its roots I cast my own roots deep; beneath its boughs
> I grow and expand; as it sighs around me in the breeze I am nourished
> with delight.[38]

[38] Cited in Bishop Kallistos Ware, 'Through the Creation to the Creator',
Third Marco Pallis Memorial Lecture, in *Ecotheology* 2 (January 1997), p. 28.

rising to a new and widened concept of self means both widen-
ing perception of who we are, and deepening a sense of responsibility within a wider relational understanding.[32] Recognising our
connectedness with each other, far from suppressing difference
(which is the usual and understandable anxiety), makes it possible
to value the ethical challenges presented by diversity and
respond to its social and political consequences. On the basis of
connection, we value difference and otherness. This has become
particularly crucial in working with Womanist Theology (the
theology of black women in the United States), with Mujerista
theologians (the theology of Hispanic women) and with
numerous groups of Third World women theologians. Paying
attention to the connections between all people has a visionary
quality (as has already been perceived in Thomas Merton's
Louisville experience).

   It is this visionary quality of the ethics of connection which
I want to stress.[33] Discovering the pattern which connects is far
from attempting to impose a false unity and uniformity on dis-
parate groups. It is not about obliterating or acquiescing in
unjust power differences. It is not about excusing horror and
tragedy by subsuming them under a wider and grander scheme –
as is frequently the case with traditional theodicies. Patient
attention to connection ushers in new visions of transcendence.
And again I quote the inspiration of Adrienne Rich:

> But there come times – perhaps this is one of them –
> when we have to take ourselves more seriously or die;
> when we have to pull back from the incantations,
> rhythms we've moved to thoughtlessly,
> and disenthrall ourselves, bestow
> ourselves to silence, or a severer listening, cleansed

[32] There is now a plethora of philosophical works on the new feminist con-
ceptualisations of self. See, for example, Morwenna Griffiths, *Feminisms
and the Self: the Web of Identity* (London: Routledge, 1995); Kathleen Lennon,
Margaret Whitford, eds, *Knowing the Difference: Feminist Perspectives in
Epistemology* (London: Routledge, 1994).
[33] See M. Grey, 'Claiming Power-in-Relation', in *Journal of Feminist Studies
in Religion*, 7(1), (1991), pp. 7–18.

  of oratory, formulas, choruses, laments, static
  crowding the wires. We cut the wires,
  find ourselves in free-fall, . . .[34]

As I hinted in the image of my grandmother weaving together the strands of our family life through carpet making, we will find a whole new poetry here in the discovery and attention to connection. As Adrienne Rich continues:

  Visions begin to happen in such a life
  as if a woman quietly walked away
  from the argument and jargon in a room
  and sitting down in the kitchen, began turning in her lap
  bits of yarn, calico and velvet scraps. . . .
  Such a composition has nothing to do with eternity,
  the striving for greatness, brilliance –
  only with the musing of a mind
  one with her body, . . .
  pulling the tenets of a life together
  with no mere will to mastery,
  only care for the many-lived, unending
  forms in which she finds herself, . . .[35]

Attending to the pattern which connects means – in an ecclesial context – being free to move away from an ethics of mastery and domination. It means attention to unheard voices, to particularity of context, and recognising responsibilities springing from this – whether this means living sustainably in the bio-region, care for all the life-forms which flourish within it, or commitment to the struggle against the many patterns of alienation, sexual oppression, dis-connection and brokennesses preventing human and non-human flourishing. Supported by a spirituality which privileges deepening the connections, a movement is enabled towards overcoming the split between knowing and feeling, between doing and thinking, theory and praxis, between re-membering the past and imagining a transformed future.

[34] Adrienne Rich, 'Transcendental Etude', in *The Dream of a Common Language* (New York: W. W. Norton, 1978), pp. 74–5.
[35] Ibid., pp. 76–7.

And within a theology where the
very energy of connectedness within
confidence to build new foundations,
heal the process of fragmentation.

Taking Wings

Relational Theology has roots – but does it
wings is to soar into the future with new vis
dom. The work of the Spirit, Holy Ruaḥ, the
ness, is always 'making all things new' even
when the movement of refugees across the
seems to have reached unimagined proportie
that humanity has learnt nothing from previou
means military power, and the adversarial ethic
we recognise. The northern hemisphere needs S
needs an enemy . . . What chance has the fragili
power at this juncture? What hope for the vulne
refugees?

  The Swedish scholar Anna Karin Hammar, in
thesis, has brought together the work of feminist
on re-imaging power, concentrating on notions o
mutuality and in mutual empowerment, the power of co
sustaining power and, of course, power in making ri
tion.[37] It is important to realise that one of the reasons for t
lock in many contentious ethical areas is a failure in imag
an imagination which is both stultified and impoverished.

  What gives us wings at this juncture is precisely the conv
that it is with the power of compassion, empathy, roote
vulnerability, that God acts; God is the power which drive
justice and makes it. If we think of the haunting lines of the prop
Hosea:

[36] For the metaphor of roots and wings I am indebted to Jay McDanie
Christianity in an Age of Dialogue – Roots and Wings (Maryknoll: Orbis, 1995).
As he explains (chapter 1) it has a long genealogy of an informal nature!
[37] See Anna Karin Hammar, *Transforming Power: Understandings of Power in Feminist Liberation Theologies* (M.Phil thesis), University of Lund, 1994.

This gives a clue to empowerment in vulnerability. For it means awareness of the power we already have. The vitality of living with awareness of connections with air, growing things and the diversity of all creatures. Learning about their vulnerability. Becoming increasingly committed to giving other creatures space. Committing our energy to where there is dynamic growth in communities of justice and withdrawing our energy from withered forms of community. Then we literally become the soil for God's action, open to the 'green grace' of healing the connections between humanity and nature, the 'red grace' of healing connections in human democratic structures, the 'golden grace' of receptivity to divine action.[39]

Even if all we do for God is to keep alternative values, possibilities and hopes alive, if we give them space we are keeping God alive in the world, embodying 'windows of vulnerability' (the phrase is Dorothee Soelle's), so that God's transforming power can act. This gives a completely different and more profound motive for keeping alive flourishing faith communities. But that means not looking to the heavens for divine thunderbolts to counteract those of Clinton, Saddam Hussein, or the guns of the Taliban in Afghanistan, but to the ghettoes and deserts of some of our inner cities, where the vulnerable God walks with her children; and it is with the words of Thomas Merton – again – that I end:

> The shadows fall. The stars appear, the birds begin to sleep. Night embraces the silent half of the earth. A vagrant, a destitute wanderer with dusty feet, finds his(her) way down a new road. A homeless God, lost in the night, without papers, without identification, without even a number, a frail expendable exile lies down in desolation under the sweet stars of the world and entrusts Herself to sleep.[40]

---

[39] 'Red' and 'green' grace are concepts cited in Jay McDaniel, *Roots and Wings*, op. cit. 'Golden' grace is my own idea.

[40] Thomas Merton, 'Hagia Sophia', in *Emblems of Fury*, cited in *The Candles are Still Burning*, M. Grey, A. Heaton, D. Sullivan, eds (London: Cassell, 1994), p. 171.

3

The 'Dark Night of the Church' as liberation of community?

Introduction

In chapter 1 it was argued that there was no way to grapple with either the process of personal self-becoming or the transformation of society without a deepening commitment to both; and that the conflict between escaping from or changing the world as played out in the tension between monastic or active Christian lifestyle is an illusory one. Merton in his hermitage, Ruether in the inner city, Julian of Norwich in her cell or Dorothy Day in her dynamic activity with the urban poor in the cities of America all break through the dualistic attempts to oppose one form of witness to another. In chapter 2 it was argued that only through a theology whose roots and wings are relational, and through communities whose lifestyle offers counter-cultural alternatives to competitive individualism and unstoppable, compulsive consumerism, has Christianity any hope of making a transformative impact on culture.

The next two chapters explore a way forward in terms of the closely intertwined dimensions of prophecy and mysticism. An attempt will be made to show how, at this moment (the run-up to the millennium), only the community which is both mystical and prophetic can develop this transformative capacity. What might this mean for what I call the 'Dark Night of the Church'? In this chapter I bring the intuitive insights of Feminist Theology on mysticism, eros, the self, into dialogue with Christian tradition; it will not be an easy journey, nor will the conclusion be easily digested. But I hope the reader will journey with me.

The Dark Night of the Church

It is probably far from clear why I am advocating a mystical way forward for the Church. Mysticism – even if the lives of both Thomas Merton and Etty Hillesum told a different story – still seems an area redolent of bright lights, private ecstasies, perhaps drug-induced hallucinations, and apparitions of the Virgin Mary! Not a phenomenon which respectable Protestants, let alone feminist theologians, could have much sympathy with! The association of these so-called mystical phenomena with certain privileged individuals throughout the history of religions has tended to give the impression that authentic religious experience is the highly intense, unmediated experience of the presence of God, often termed 'ineffable', even if the mark of the mystics concerned has been an unbreakable determination to communicate the content of their visions and divine messages.

Recently we have seen many attacks on such a notion of religious experience. First, it is a very private notion of experience, usually associated with the analysis of William James, who saw religious experience as 'heightened states of private feeling'.[1] Nicholas Lash, in his critical study of religious experience, *Easter in Ordinarie*, takes James to task for identifying personal experience with individual experience, for assuming that there is such a thing as pure experience, and for not understanding that so-called private experience is not innocent, not naked, not unencumbered by a person's worlds of universes – customs, patterns of thought, gender, social conditions or relative state of power and powerlessness.[2] By calling the bluff of this privatised notion, Lash's incisive critique opens a window of hope that a wider understanding of mysticism is a possibility for Christian discipleship:

[1] See William James, *The Varieties of Religious Experience* (cited in chapter 1).
[2] Op. cit., chapters 2-4.

It earlier seems as though James's tendency to speak as if only a small number of unusual, gifted, or perhaps deranged individuals possess the equipment that could enable them personally to experience a relationship with the Divine, left the rest of us out in the cold, cut off from God. But we are not, as supposed, as badly off as we supposed. For, whatever can be said about James's 'mothersea' of 'co-consciousness', I cannot think of any reasons for mistaking it for the mystery of God.[3]

The feminist theologian Grace Jantzen is equally critical of James' restriction of mystical experience to the private world of the individual.[4] In addition, she makes us aware of a gendered dimension in the way mystical experiences are described. For example, the image of the 'ladder' is never found in the descriptions of the visions of female mystics;[5] her inference is that women are less bound up with hierarchical structures, hence less inclined to use metaphors of ascent as automatically implying superiority; this is an element to which I need to return in the discussion on community and mysticism.

Thirdly, Denys Turner, in his recent study, *The Darkness of God: Negativity in Christian Mysticism*,[6] is even more forthrightly critical of what modern writers call 'mysticism'; the medieval mystics would even call this *anti-mysticism*, he says, in the sense

---

[3] Ibid., p. 81.

[4] Grace Jantzen, *Power, Gender and Mysticism* (cited in chapter 1). This is a central theme in her book. In the concluding chapter she writes: 'Far from being a neutral, objective account, the Jamesian account of mysticism accepted by modern philosophers of religion is an account inextricably intertwined with issues of power and gender in ways which feminists need to deconstruct. The privatised, subjectivised ineffable mysticism of William James and his followers is open to women as well as men; but it plays directly into the hands of modern bourgeois political and gender assumptions. It keeps God (and women) safely out of politics and the public realm; it allows mysticism to flourish as a secret inner life, while those who nurture such an inner life can generally be counted on to prop up rather than challenge the status quo of their workplaces, their gender roles, and the political systems by which they are governed, since their anxieties and angers will be allayed in the privacy of their own hearts' search for peace and tranquillity' (p. 346).

[5] Jantzen, in conversation.

[6] Denys Turner, *The Darkness of God* (cited in chapter 1).

that they would deny that metaphors of ascent, union and in-wardness refer to *states of subjective feeling*.[7] In fact, whereas con-temporary writers (following James) appear to have psychologised these metaphors, the 'medieval writer used the metaphors in an "apophatic" spirit, to play down the value of the "experiential"' (p. 4).

But it is one thing to decry an individualising and psychologi-sing of the phenomena of religious experience – even within a theology deliberately relational! – and quite another to enthrone the community as mystic. The starting point is an exploration of the best-known mystical metaphor, namely, the *Dark Night*, but here I use it to describe the situation in which the Church finds itself in relation to the contemporary world.

I begin with a recent experience in the University of Nijmegen, The Netherlands. I was exploring with students the need for justice-seeking communities; these communities, we hoped, would have eucharistic celebrations linked with concern for the environ-ment; their ethical commitments would include eradicating every form of oppression that could be imagined; central would be the activity of 'visioning', so as to honour the dreams of the whole people. Yet, when I asked the question, 'How do we do this on the basis of the churches we know?', there was an emphatic rejection of the question itself. So great was the students' experience of estrangement, that they all (all doctoral level students) saw the pursuit of truth and justice as taking place *outside the experience of all the Churches*.

What had gone wrong? Admittedly The Netherlands has had a particularly bruising experience of relations with the hierarchy since the late 1960s, and especially since the death of Cardinal Alfrink was followed by the appointment of conservative bishops by the Vatican. Yet, of course, the force of the students' bitterness was also linked with the Roman Catholic Church's treatment of women; sadly, two generations of estrangement will take years of healing. So I was always conscious while teaching in The Netherlands that as long as I concentrated on justice issues,

7 Ibid., p. 44.

or on a spirituality which, although political, did not concern itself with church structures and authority (even if critical of them), I was listened to.

But there comes a point when care for justice includes care for the institution; I am convinced that to pretend that we could do without institutions and the structures and practices which maintain them, in favour of loosely prophetic groups on the margins, is not only an illusory hope, but would be élitist in the extreme. Yet it is undeniable that we are in the midst of a real crisis. I described one situation from within the Roman Catholic Church, but we could multiply examples from across the denominations. Do the Churches speak a language which offers hope to the violent young people on the streets or in the schools? Why has the Church been silent until recently about violence against women? About clergy abuse of children? About racism? Why is eucharistic hospitality not offered to gay communities? Are church liturgies experienced as shrines of boredom? Whereas there is *some* joint ecclesial action on poverty, homelessness and asylum cases, and there has been some specific criticism of the lottery money, the question of becoming the kind of countercultural communities who live by a different ethic is seldom voiced. (I realise that there are important exceptions to this, of which the Iona community in Scotland and the Taizé community in the South of France, are shining examples; these are sources of inspiration that ecclesial community does offer a way forward.)

So it seemed to me that it was the metaphor of darkness, negativity, the *Dark Night of the Church* which best captured our situation – hence the title of my book, where I explore what Christian community would have to become to recover from this impasse.[8] Here I focus on the Church in two key dimensions – the mystical and the prophetic. I want to move the metaphor of the Dark Night out of the cell of Julian of Norwich, out of Merton's hermitage and John of the Cross' prison, into the violent ghettoes of the inner city, the humiliated despair of our overcrowded

---

[8] M. Grey, *Beyond the Dark Night?* (London: Geoffrey Chapman, 1997).

47

prisons, the hopelessness of the ravaged women in the refuges. This is the sense in which the lostness, pain and confusion of Dark Night metaphor fits a situation where the Church has lost its way and seems incapable of making an adequate response. This is not because of a lack of personal goodness in many of its leaders. Nor because there have not been wise documents written, full of good sense on many social topics.[9] Nor even because of the hierarchy itself, the usual whipping-post of feminist theologians. My argument has never been that women should replace men, that he's should become she's, Fathers turn into Mothers. I think that fundamentally the Church has lost its way as regards prophecy and mysticism (seen here as the Way of Darkness, the Via Negativa).[10] We have gone as far as we can go in exalting the saintly individuals – the Mother Teresas, the Archbishop Romeros and martyrs of El Salvador, contemporary saints, missionaries and visionaries. Of course, it is good to honour people and hold them up as role models. It will continue to be a cherished part of our worship. But to some extent this has had a disempowering effect: the hero/heroine mould idealises the individual concerned, who becomes a cult figure (in fact this has already happened to Thomas Merton). Not only do their achievements seem unattainable by ordinary mortals, but they distract from the community taking responsibility for its own witness.

How could the Via Negativa, the contemplative way, the mystical path, offer any light in this darkness?

I said to my soul, be still . . .

You must go by a way wherein there is no ecstasy.
In order to arrive at what you do not know
You must go by a way which is the way of ignorance . . .[11]

---

[9] The most recent document of the Catholic Bishops' Conference, *The Common Good* (Gabriel Communications, 1996), is a good instance of this.

[10] This, of course, has made a comeback in Matthew Fox's Creation Spirituality. See *Original Blessing* (Santa Fe: Bear & Co., 1981).

[11] T. S. Eliot, 'East Coker', in *The Four Quartets* (London: Faber & Faber, 1944), p. 201.

Thus said Eliot bleakly, certainly adverting to the confusion and lostness at the heart of the Dark Night. I need to clarify that I use the phrase in many senses, deliberately playing on ambiguity. First, there is a Jungian interpretation of darkness as the shadow side of ourselves, needing integration. A recent article by a clinical psychologist, Mary Dunn, asked what exactly are the shadow aspects of Church?', which she suggests are repressed, only to emerge in destructive ways:

> They are the unacknowledged, unloved and unhealthy aspects of our ecclesiastical life together. In a family the shadow is what we colloquially think of as 'skeletons in the cupboard'. They are the events, memories, remarks, relationships and suspicions which hurt when we think about them. The shadow parts of the light and dark of our lives are the departure from our professed standards. Could the powerful people in the church who use silencing as a form of control make their actions public? . . . An unmistakeable characteristic of shadow is that it cannot be spoken; if it is named it must be faced, and an unhealthy system will seek to avoid to do so.[12]

In a healthy system, she continues, the sacrament of community 'allows us to descend into the dark wet humus of the earth together and genuinely encounter there our own rejected selves in the person of those we reject, so that we can rise with the risen Lord' (ibid.). Instead of this, she continues, a closed system maintains itself through fear, imposed secrecy and silence, deifying the past to maintain the status quo, 'in order to prevent the emergence of disturbing new ideas'. So, much in the same way that I call us to recognise where we are as the place of the Dark Night, she calls on us to stay with our shadow side and work with agonising issues.

But, secondly, there is an extremely urgent and practical side of the Dark Night. As I wrote in my book *Redeeming the Dream:*

---

[12] Mary Dunn, 'The Church's Shadow Side', in *The Tablet*, 27 July 1996, pp. 980–1.

> The feminist cry 'Take back the Night' is a demand to be able to walk freely and with safety in darkness, without fear of attack and violation. For the truth is, that for young children, both boys and girls, and for women, the night is no longer theirs.[13]

But 'Take back the Night', like embracing our shadow side, is also a call to reclaim and redeem our spiritual heritage. Mary Giles, author of *The Feminist Mystic*, writes:

> We only claim a night that is the spiritual birthright of every person, irrespective of sex or profession, a night that is ours but that for want of adequate commentary from the point of view of women today may seem to be the exclusive property of theologians and cloistered religious.[14]

Let me take this further. Whereas the despair is real – about violence on the streets, or about discrimination and injustice within the Church – the impasse of the Dark Night is experienced at an even deeper level:

> The Dark Night comprehends a much deeper level of alienation and despair. It is a darkness born of a lack of nourishment in the liturgy, prayer life and doctrine . . . It is the pain of the distorted symbols and lifeless rituals . . . ; it is the making of the Christ mystery into something un-related to human living and the controlling of this by a clerical élite . . . it is having no form of prayer which connects with one's life experience, having the life of the Spirit choked back and still-born . . . The total impasse of the night, the experience of being made mute and inarticulate – not in the silence of loving contemplation, but because the language sought for has not yet been brought to birth – descends with shocking immediacy.[15]

What I was exploring in my earlier book was the need to hang on in there, in full acknowledgement of the darkness, lostness and pain of being let down by the very wellsprings of Christian nourishment. Janet Morley's psalms express this act of faith in

---

[13] M. Grey, *Redeeming the Dream*, p. 79.

[14] Mary E. Giles, 'Take back the Night' in Mary Giles, ed., *The Feminist Mystic* (New York: Crossroad, 1982), pp. 39–70, quotation p. 39.

[15] Grey, op. cit., pp. 75–7.

the darkness very beautifully; this psalm is entitled 'I will praise God, my Beloved' and refers to the presence of God at the centre of all lostness:

> Even in chaos you will bear me up;
> if the waters go over my head,
> you will still be holding me.
>
> For the chaos is yours also,
> and in the swirling of mighty waters
> is your presence known.[16]

But what I referred to earlier on the level of the individual, I now urge at the level of the institution. At the personal level we wait, we pay attention to all the many connections, the disordered patterns of relation, hearkening (to use Etty Hillesum's phrase), listening, discerning, pulling back from rhythms we've moved to thoughtlessly (I recall here the words of Adrienne Rich in 'Transcendental Etude')[17] – in other words, practising a 'spirituality of attention' (which, of course, Simone Weil has made famous).[18] Because of the level of confusion, grief and sense of betrayal I think we can reclaim a maxim of an even older spirituality, cited

---

[16] Janet Morley, 'I Will Praise God, My Beloved', *All Desires Known* (London: Women in Theology, 1988), p. 50.

[17] See chapter 2.

[18] Simone Weil, *Waiting on God* (London, Fontana, 1951), tr. Emma Crawford. In 'Reflections on the Right Use of School Studies', p. 72, she wrote: 'Attention consists of suspending our thought, leaving it detached, empty and ready to be penetrated by the object. . . . Above all, our thought should be empty, waiting, not seeking anything, but ready to receive in its naked truth the object which seeks to penetrate it.' In 'Forms of the Implicit Love of God', p. 149, she gives this a more explicitly spiritual interpretation: 'The activity which brings about salvation is not like any form of activity. The Greek word which expresses it is *hypomene*, and *patientia* is rather an inadequate translation of it. It is the waiting or attentive and faithful immobility which lasts indefinitely and cannot be shaken. The slave, who waits near the door so as to open immediately the master knocks, is the best image of it. He must be ready to die of hunger and exhaustion rather than change his attitude.' Although it would be possible to make a feminist critique of both these passages, to do so would be to miss the profound spiritual point of a spirituality of waiting and attention.

in the moving book of the late Gillian Rose, *Love's Work*: 'Keep your mind in hell, and despair not . . .' She continues: 'The Tradition is far kinder in its understanding that to live, to love, is to be failed, to be forgiven, for ever and ever. Keep your mind in Hell and despair not.'[19]

But we stay in this place of pain for the sake of the Church, for community, for new patterns of relating, out of fidelity to the Spirit, who is the very energy of relation, connection and the vitality of all living things. Not out of a sense of self-inflicted injury, or a futile wallowing in despair, but, first, out of a sense of compassion with the vulnerable God, a ministry to 'bear up God in the world' (the root meaning of compassion),[20] and because of the conviction that there is a new way of being Church (or an old one, reclaimed) and this is the only way it will be born. So, 'I said to my soul, be still' is not the stillness of opting out, of despair, but a free, communally-chosen act of hoping.

But if this is the mystical way, *the Way of Darkness*, how does it represent a rereading of the mystical tradition, particularly of John of the Cross' 'Dark Night of the Soul'? I will first look at the meaning of negativity in the context of the apophatic way, mindful of Denys Turner's critique of the tradition, and then propose a rereading of this, in the light of a forgotten dimension, namely, the tragic. Then the way will be open to reclaim the prophetic heart of community.

[19] Gillian Rose, *Love's Work* (London: Chatto & Windus 1995), p. 98. She died not long after this was published.

[20] See Carter Heyward, *Our Passion for Justice* (cited in chapter 1), p. 206: 'The root meaning of passion or suffering – *passio* – is to bear, to withstand, to hold up. We are called, collectively, to bear up God in the world. To withstand/stand with is to be in solidarity with God, to bear up God in the world, to go with God in our comings and goings. This vocation involves pain, as Jeremiah, Jesus, and all bearers of God have known – but not only pain. To be passionate lovers of human beings, the earth, and other earth creatures; to love passionately the God who is Godself, the resource of this love is to participate in an inspired and mind-bogglingly delightful way of moving collectively in history.'

Surrendering to darkness.

This is possibly the most difficult part of the argument, where I try to bring together the sense of waiting, in darkness, as a way forward for the Church, with the intuition of being on the brink of a new way of being Church, and against the background of the rejection of the notion of mysticism as subjective states of feeling confined to a privileged élite. As a starting point a few lines of another of Janet Morley's psalms will serve as inspiration:

> And there was no terror   only stillness
> and I was wanting nothing and
> it was fullness and it was like aching for God
> and it was touch and warmth and
> darkness and no time and no words and we flowed . . .
> and I was given up to the dark and
> in the darkness   I was not lost
> and the wanting was like fullness . . .[21]

Such can be the startling effect of this poem that it goes against the grain to analyse what is going on here; but the poem brings a new element to the discussion. Clearly an erotic experience is being described, yes, of darkness, but also of longing, surrender, akin to aching for God. It highlights what was already hinted at in the first chapter – the mystics' use of eros, desire, longing, with definite sexual connotations, which evokes an embodied form of mysticism. Here is an example from the Flemish mystic, the thirteenth-century Béguine, Hadewych:

> To those who give themselves thus to content Love,
> What great wonders shall happen!
> With love they shall cleave in oneness to Love,
> and with love they shall contemplate all Love –
> Drawing through her secret veins,
> On the channel where love gives all love,
> and inebriates her drunken friends with love

---

[21] Janet Morley, op. cit., 'And You Held Me', p. 56.

> In amazement before her violence:
> This remains wholly hidden from aliens,
> but well-known to the wise.[22]

If Sarah Coakley is right that we should turn Freud's dictum upside down, that instead of God-talk being about sex, rather sex is about God, then eros language is absolutely appropriate in expressing the journey to God.[23] The language of eros, found of course in Dionysius and in Eckhart, is here most explicit: only through desire, through longing, can one reach Love itself. But God's longing, God's desire is ontologically prior. . . . How does this fit, then, with the denial of mysticism as mere subjective states of feeling and the emphasis on emptying, negativity and the apophatic way?

First, Turner must be right that the Dark Night of the Soul which John of the Cross describes is truly the harrowing process 'which must be undergone by those to whom God comes more than averagely close'.[24] There simply is no easy way. Are we reassured by knowing that God is the initiator of the process, drawing the soul towards greater love and delight? When we put this fact alongside the vulnerability of God which I have been exploring? Turner discusses the problem in terms of the different levels of selfhood. He discerns the *psychological* self (which is the self of ordinary experience), the *therapeutic* self (which tells us, in states of depression, that something is wrong), and the *self of numerical identity*, which is simply a guarantee of continuing identity (I would call it the self of convenience).[25] The strength of the metaphor of

[22] Hadewych, 'To Bear the Yoke', stanza 6, in *Hadewych: The Complete Works*, tr. and introd. Mother Columba Hart OSB (New York: Paulist Press, 1980), p. 159.

[23] Sarah Coakley, 'Batter My Heart: Feminist Reorientations of Trinitarian Thought', in *The Three-personed God* (The Hulsean Lectures 1992).

[24] Turner, op. cit., p. 231.

[25] Ibid., p. 228. One of the best discussions on the difference between self and person is found in Catherine Keller, *From a Broken Web*, especially chapter 4, 'The Selves of Psyche'. Building on insights from the process thought of Alfred North Whitehead, she describes the person as a series of many self-moments, so that 'person' becomes an umbrella term for gathering them together. This itself is beautifully grounded in the God/person relation: 'A self is a node in the

negativity is to emphasise the poverty of our notions of self. Turner then distinguishes between active and passive dark nights.[26] The point of the active Dark Night is to do the best we can and through ascetic practices to construct an autonomous and selfcontrolled notion of selfhood (p. 237). This is the *ascetical self*, which is, as he admits, a somewhat priggish construction. But the passive Dark Nights are something different: they

> are the dawning of the realisation that in this loss of selfhood, nothing is lost; it is the awakening of the capacity to live without the need for it . . . but what is lost in the passive dark nights was never the self at all, but only an illusion all along. (p. 244)

So it is *possessive selfhood* which poses the problem. Strategies of the Dark Night, concludes Turner, 'are the divine strategies of detachment, . . . not merely from a particular self-of-experience, but of the need for a self-of-experience of any kind' (ibid.).

Now it seems to me that we have to put these notions of the way of purgation (the Via Purgativa), described by the mystics as preparing the ground for union with God, with two other elements. In our present Dark Night of the Church, given the starvation of nourishment, ('eucharistic famine', as Rosemary Ruether has called it),[27] forsakenness and confusion, it is exactly the possessive self which is being whittled away. Add to that the experience of many women, poor people, mentally handicapped people, Aids sufferers, of being 'no-thing', non-being, sub-human, and there is a social context of no-self here missed both by the medieval mystics and most contemporary interpreters. Feminism is extraordinarily active around the careful construction of identity, according to

---

network of world, and in each self is an Eros ensouling the world. The world has heart – where we embrace the Universe as condensed, personified, particularised, in those metaphors of the sacred that inspire us. If we meet God in ourselves, we meet her at the molten core of heart's desire, ever again energising our courage and our quest' (pp. 214–15).

[26] Turner is gender-blind in this analysis. As this point is well discussed by Jantzen (*Power, Gender and Mysticism*, op. cit.), here I take it as read and do not discuss it further.

[27] Rosemary Ruether, *Women Church* (New York: Harper & Row, 1989), p. 4.

gender, race, culture and economic position.[28] When, in chapter 1, I brought this search for the widened concept of self into dialogue with Thomas Merton's stripping away of the illusory self, possessive self, I looked for resolution of the tension in terms of the visionary quality of the connected self.

But the connected self is not an identity that remains fixed. It is constantly being made and re-made through the very epiphanies of connection which are the stuff of community experience. The willingness to reconstruct identity as we die to our own racism, nationalism, heterosexism and allow other groups their place in the sun, is part of the challenge. (For example, the aftermath of the war in Bosnia poses the urgent challenge of recognising the identity and needs of the Muslim communities, in the wake of atrocities and rapes; the fact of their being regarded as 'other' must be seen as having provided some pretext for such horrors.)

It cannot be the darkness of non-being, discrimination, home-lessness, being forced into refugee status, which is meant by the death of self of the Dark Night. That is a naive romanticism cloaking real injustice. It is this very non-being which is evoking a 'mysticism of resistance' in the name of the justice and peace of the Kingdom of God. Non-being, kept in place as ideology by the false idols of the God of power and might, is being confronted by us calling out, with Meister Eckhart, 'I pray God to rid me of God'. And this is why God has become vulnerable for us and with us, this frail, homeless God of the gutters whom Etty Hillesum wanted to make at home, even on her way to Auschwitz. This is why, even in this the Dark Night, there is a growing yearning for God, a new language of eros is arising, and the tentative expressions – of which Janet Morley's poem is but one – of a language and symbolism to articulate our hunger for wholeness, an end to violence and the ravaging of the earth.

[28] See Morwenna Griffiths, *Feminisms and the Self: the Web of Identity* (London and New York: Routledge, 1995); Kathleen Lennon and Margaret Whitford, eds, *Knowing the Difference: Feminist Perspectives in Epistemology* (London and New York: Routledge, 1995); Mary McClintock Fulkerson, *Changing the Subject: Women's Discourses and Feminist Theology* (Minneapolis: Fortress, 1994).

But what I want to hang onto in terms of John of the Cross' process is this: the intuition that we respond to God's eros with our own longing is a sure one; but this desiring, yearning for God will lead us into darkness. Sarah Coakley, commenting on Gregory of Nyssa's *Life of Moses*, is sure that Gregory is telling us that advance toward intimacy with God will lead to an 'unnerving darkness', the darkness of incomprehensibility.[29] Journey into God is, after all, journey into mystery. Secondly, as a community seeking a way forward together, this is the only place to be and the only way to go. There is no other way. And the breakthrough will come through the way of surrender – not to the forces of non-being, destructive of the fragile self of the most rejected categories of society, but surrender to God's initiative. Constance Fitzgerald writes that this will be the fruit of unconscious processes:

> The psychologists and the theologians, the poets and the mystics, assure us that impasse can be the condition for creative growth, and transformation, if the experience of impasse is fully appropriated within one's heart and flesh with consciousness and consent; if the limitations of one's humanity and the human condition are squarely faced and the limits of one's finitude allowed to invade the human spirit with real existential powerlessness.[30]

This has been a difficult theme to articulate: the purpose has been to reclaim the contemplative way as the way of waiting, hoping, longing during what is experienced as the Dark Night of the Church. I have tried to rescue the mystical way from the threat of privatised individual subjectivity, yet to restore to it the experience of hunger and yearning which is emerging in this famine of nourishment, together with recovering a practical meaning of non-self which is not to be idealised or defended either by theologian or politician. It was to rescue those who dwell in the twilight of our structures that God became human in the first place.

---

[29] Coakley, op. cit., p. 42.

[30] Constance Fitzgerald, 'Impasse and the Dark Night', in Joann Wolski Conn, ed., *Women's Spirituality: Resources for Development* (New Jersey: Paulist Press, 1986), p. 290.

There is one final point, which is again far from easy. That God is vulnerable, to be discovered in the soil of our vulnerability to each other, our openness to connection and right relation, is a hard saying. It does not seem to inspire hope. But I think that it looks different from a tragic reading of our tradition. This is a highly unpopular reading in a tradition which is firmly hooked to the idea of cosmic victory. Kathleen Sands, an American feminist theologian, criticises feminist theologians (in particular, Rosemary Ruether and Carol Christ) for not paying attention to the tragic,[31] although I felt that her book failed to show us exactly what difference that would make to the way we shape our lives, if we took the tragic seriously. In general, the concern for order, for goodness to have the final word, for the unthinking trust in what is loosely termed 'progress', and for a clear-cut right and wrong about every issue, can make us blind to the significance of the ambiguity, messiness and tragic happenings in life. It is a dimension which the Greek tragedies portray sharply, as the philosopher Martha Nussbaum saw clearly in her book, *The Fragility of Goodness*,[32] and the spiritual writer Simone Weil saw even more clearly.[33]

My hunch is that with a tragic reading of at least some of our spiritual sources, we may gain a clue as to why the Dark Night is perennially with us, and why the way *through* (not *out of* the darkness) is to recognise our vulnerability. It has always been there for us to see (but perhaps we did not want to) that whatever causal explanations we find for illnesses, earthquakes, accidents, famines, wars – and I know we must keep on doing so, and being honest about our human culpability – yet at the end of the day it remains tragic that innocent people die, innocent children are murdered,

---

[31] Kathleen Sands, *Evil and Tragedy in Feminist Theology* (Minneapolis: Fortress, 1994). See also M. Grey, *The Wisdom of Fools?*, chapter 9, 'Evil and Theodicy'. It is one of the criticisms of process thought – which sprang from the climate of evolutionary theory – that it depends on a certain optimism as regards growth and progress.

[32] Martha Nussbaum, *The Fragility of Goodness* (Oxford University Press, 1986).

[33] See Katherine T. Brueck, *The Redemption of Tragedy: The Literary Vision of Simone Weil* (New York: SUNY, 1995).

thousands of elderly people live out their days in poverty and loneliness, and that the continent of Africa seems beset by insoluble problems of hunger and war. And that is only to speak about the macro level; in addition, all human beings struggle with their own personal tragedies.

Perhaps our human desire to find explanations and therefore to control is one of the mechanisms by which we block an under-standing of the tragic dimension. It is often only through drama, poetry and music that its poignancy hits us. But our own faith sources are permeated with a sense of tragedy. Where do we find the tragic in God more powerfully expressed than in the lament of the Prophet Micah,

> 'O my people, what have I done to you?
> In what have I wearied you?
> Answer me.' (Micah 6.3)

This is the very passage which found new interpretation in the Christian Good Friday worship, the Reproaches.[34] The theme of suffering and pain in God has become common currency since Moltmann's book, *The Suffering God*,[35] and Kazoh Kitamori's *The Pain of God*;[36] yet the dimension of tragedy in God has always seemed to be in direct opposition to the goodness of creation. But suppose we reread the gospel accounts of the ministry of Jesus, understanding him as a human being fully conscious of this tragic dimension – Jesus weeping over Jerusalem, grieved over the death of the only son of a widow, grieving over the death of a beloved friend, Lazarus; Jesus who said 'Take up your cross daily and follow me' not to glorify suffering as the only way to wear the badge of being Christian, not to keep the poor as poor and despised, but because there would always be tragedy, loss and grief. Then his own death can be seen as the paradigmatic tragedy of the killing of innocent life. So if we read the injunction to die to self in order to find new life in full consciousness of the tragic, this does not mean

---

[34] In the new liturgy of the Roman Catholic Church, sadly, the Reproaches have been dropped.

[35] Jürgen Moltmann, *The Suffering God* (London: SCM, 1973, ET 1974).

[36] Kazoh Kitamori, *Theology of the Pain of God* (London: SCM, 1965).

denying eros, pleasure, joy, and joy-in-relation; it is to say that there will always be a constant dying to self through engagement with life in its fullness. But his message is that *God is in it too*, sharing our vulnerability, leaving the high towers of patriarchy, the bastions producing the weaponry of destruction. But humanity in its deafness refuses to learn. How many times must it be said that 'God died in Auschwitz' for us to understand that our images of God, and the human constructions which we base on them, are idols to be let go of? That is why we are continually plunged back to the Dark Night. It is not final solutions we have been promised, but the faithfulness of God, the justice of God, and most of all that eros of God which is the only power we want in this shared darkness of our communities. As Hadewych put it:

> To all who desire love, may God grant
> That they be so prepared for Love
> that they all live on her riches
> Until after themselves becoming Love,
> they draw Love into themselves
> So that nothing evil, on the part of cruel aliens,
> Can befall them more; but they shall live free
> To cry: I am all Love's, and Love is all mine!
> what can disturb them?
> For under Love's power stand
> The sun, moon, and stars![37]

But, lest the reader think that he or she is abandoned in the darkness, contemplating the tragic dimension, the good news is that this is a very active place to be – but for that we need the prophetic dimension. And that is another story.

---

[37] Hadewych, op. cit., Stanza 7, p. 159.

4

꧁꙳꧂

Children of Sophia and the community as prophet

Introduction

In this final chapter I reach the real core for which I have been preparing: how do we act out of the prophetic and mystical heart of community so as to offer alternatives to the prevailing ethos of competitive individualism and instrumental hedonism? How could this prophetic heart of community shine with this hope in the Dark Night I began to describe in chapter 3? In focusing here on action, I will explore the following questions:

- What kind of prophecy is needed today?
- What kind of action will it inspire? (I focus on two examples)

And, finally,

- What revelation of the Holy Ruaḥ (Spirit) of God is refuelling the prophetic heart of community?

I begin by asking, 'What is the image of the prophet which prevails?' A certain caricature springs to mind, namely, the bearded Jeremiah character bemoaning the morals of the times – and there certainly have been many of these. That the Jeremiahs were also fired by visions of justice, steeped in the wisdom of their faith communities, empowered by the Holy Ruaḥ of God with their own mystical faith, is frequently ignored. If I asked who are the comparable contemporary figures, suggestions would perhaps include Gandhi and his great vision of non-violence, Martin Luther King, the controversial Mother Teresa, Dag Hammarskjøld,

Dorothy Day, the Abbé Pierre, Bob Geldof at the time of the Ethiopian famine, the Jewish writer Eli Wiesel, the Berrigan brothers who burned the draft papers in opposition to the Vietnam war, Petra Kelly, prophet of the Green Party, perhaps President Aristide of Haiti, Oscar Romero of El Salvador . . . Encouragingly, there is no lack of courageous women and men challenging the *zeitgeist* and prepared to die to keep alive the flicker of hope.

But this is a time when – as I hinted in the case of the mystics – reliance merely on outstanding figures is not only insufficient but could even be counter-productive in an individualist culture. We have gone as far as we can go with this model. If 'to be is to relate', to be in process, movement, it is in the quality of the *community as prophet* that our hope must be situated. By all means let us give honour to women and men of courage, but let us also take the responsibility of becoming the kinds of communities which challenge society and live by a transforming ethic, communities which 'shine like stars' because they are 'offering the word of life' (1 Peter).

What kind of group will be seen as counter-cultural?

But the first objection will be that sects, as opposed to Churches (to take the typology of Troeltsch), have done exactly this. Many sects do offer an alternative in world-despising contexts where, in a severe ethos of no alcohol, drugs or pub-culture, their adherents live in strictly-defined communities where interaction with the world at large is severely curtailed and where sexual relationships are usually centrally controlled and firmly within the options of marriage or celibacy. I am here speaking about a range of Christian groupings, since there is a fluidity between the Church/sect groupings found in a variety of House-Church movements,[1]

[1] For House Church movements, see Andrew Walker, *Restoring the Kingdom* (London: Hodder & Stoughton, 1977). I leave out of the present discussion the more sinister form of sects, associated with brainwashing youngsters, controlling them, and gaining access to any funds they may possess.

Adventist Groups, and charismatic and pentecostalist groups across the denominations. Many are fundamentalist in their reading of Scripture and tradition – but even here there are enormous differences. I think this option has to be taken seriously as it is the fastest-growing Christian reaction to the permissive, promiscuous and consumptive society about which I have been speaking. And in certain Third World countries like Nicaragua and Chile, Pentecostalism is growing far faster in what is per-ceived as the failure of Liberation Theology to deliver its promises. Nearer at home, revivalism in Southampton (where I live in England) has reached enormous proportions.

My closest experience with one of these groups was in Belgium, in Brussels, where the charismatic movement The Word of God (now renamed Jerusalem) has been active since the late 1970s. Avowedly ecumenical, it is closely related to the Roman Catholic Church,[2] even regarding itself as a prophetic community of the end times. Many of these sect-like groups have an end-time consciousness; if both Church and society collapse because of the sinfulness of the times, they will come into their own as the true Church. Here the lifestyle of the members is built around strong family groupings, in deliberate recreation of the house churches of the early Church based on the witness of the Acts of the Apostles. Most of its members have normal jobs (although women are encouraged to fulfil traditional home-making functions), but their free time is organised completely around the movement, with either prayer evenings or 'community days' and a climax on Sundays. The interpretation of Scripture is conservative, bordering on fundamentalist. For example, the role of the father in the family is crucial: he has authority over wife and children, and in addi-tion is the spiritual leader, regarded as having special communi-cation with God (this is of course on the basis of a certain reading of Pauline theology). The woman's role is derivative and dependent on his. Added to this, the liturgies are strictly of a charismatic type, with an emphasis on praise, prophecy and speaking in tongues;

---

[2] The growth of the charismatic movement in Belgium owes much to the influ-ence of the late Cardinal Suenens.

charitable activity – of which there is a considerable amount – is focused within the community.

I think we should not underestimate the positive points of such a grouping. In times when the traditional family structure has clearly changed, if not broken down together with even basic traditional morality, I see this group as providing a structure and discipline that gives people of all age ranges a quality experience of community belonging, beyond what they could have imagined. The sheer affection and commitment to community members, the quality of support systems set up, the enthusiasm of the liturgies – this is not lightly to be underestimated. I know many young people set on fire for Christianity, many older people whose marriages were rocky, whose faith was lukewarm or tired, whose lives have been completely regenerated. In the larger scheme of things, these groups have a valued place.

But are they what is needed as prophetic communities today? If I return to the theme of chapter 1, 'Escape the world or change the world?', what I tried to argue was the false dichotomy of this challenge, and that any full-blooded Christian faith needed to grapple with all the social and material realities of society, whether from the hermit's cell or the inner city ghettoes. Not for nothing did the theologian Mark Kline Taylor construct a Christology around the notion 'Christus Mater',[3] Christ as mother. He did not mean to identify Christ with mothers, but to show that any understanding of Christ today – indeed, any contemporary Christology – must reflect the economic and material realities which are the bedrock of the lives of poor women. In chapter 2 I argued for a relational theology in which the very structures of faith and understanding of God were deeply-rooted in the making of justice in society; it is impossible to separate the journey to personal holiness from struggles against the powers which keep poverty, sexism and racism in place. So within a mystical faith which awaits the end of the Dark Night of injustice, prophetic community means groups who engage holistically with the forces which keep the Dark

[3] Mark Kline Taylor, *Remembering Esperanza: A Cultural Political Theology for N. American Praxis* (Maryknoll: Orbis, 1993).

Night in being. I want now to explore what kind of prophecy is called for in this situation and what kind of prophetic action is needed: is the conflict between institutional and prophetic elements inevitable? I will end by exploring an insight of chapter 1, where I cited Merton on the figure of Sophia: how could a recovery of Sophia and of the sophianic wisdom traditions enable the recovery of the prophetic and mystical heart of community?

Renewing the heart of prophecy

> We need to intervene for one another. We need a new world view that puts the old one 'in new light'. But how? And where will this spirituality of contemplative co-creation come from in this indi-vidualistic culture? And in what way can the religious leaders of our time help build this bridge from privatized piety to public moral responsibility? I suggest that . . . we begin to look at the bases of social brokenness . . . that we ourselves begin to see the link between the personal and political.[4]

I begin with three images and then explore three dimensions of what prophecy might mean today. The first is of the writer, Joan Chittester, from whom the above quotation was taken. She is a Benedictine Prioress from Erie, Pennsylvania, and in 1995 joined the Peace Train from Helsinki to Beijing to participate in the UN International Conference on Women. Two hundred and thirty women from forty-two different countries travelled the 6,000 miles to China, holding discussions and seminars on the way with women's groups in St Petersburg, the Ukraine, Bucharest, Sofia (Bulgaria), Odessa, Kazakhstan and China itself. What the journey dramatically revealed, and the Peace Train delegation startlingly showed (as Joan Chittester wrote in a poignantly honest travel diary), was

> the silent linkage between women and violence everywhere. It is women and children who are the real victims of war, the silent casual-ties of militarism, the invisible scapegoats of budget cuts made to

---

[4] Joan Chittester, *Woman Strength: Modern Church, Modern Woman* (London: Sheed & Ward, 1990), pp. 69–70.

enhance the budgets of the world, the bleeding quarry of the rapes now defined as legitimate weapons of the war machine. It is women and children who suffer most from the wars men fight to 'defend' them.[5]

But equally moving for her was the experience of being with a community of women committed to justice, a community which built up and strengthened as the train snaked its way from country to country, revealing in a diversity of political and social settings the desperate and increasing poverty of women.

Yet prophecy must be about keeping hope alive, and my next image expresses this. In July 1996, 1,000 women met at Gmünden, Austria, to participate in the first European Women's Synod. It was an event which affirmed the authority of women as active decision-makers. Amid all the resolutions which were passed resisting injustice in numerous ways in both Church and society, the most powerful experience was that of solidarity. It was symbolised by the closing liturgy in which Christian, Jewish, Muslim, Hindu, and women from goddess spirituality groups, together with many secular women (and including many from post-communist countries), recommissioned each other in the communal search for truth and justice, and sang over and over again, 'Sister, carry on, it may be rocky and it may be rough, But sister, carry on.'[6]

My third experience comes from my own involvement in India in the villages of Rajasthan, as part of a project bringing water to a drought-stricken area.[7] Part of the learning experience from this project is that the obvious truism that 'water gives life' takes on new dimensions. When wells are constructed in a village and

[5] Joan Chittester, *Beyond Beijing: The Next Step for Women* (London: Sheed & Ward, 1996), pp. 1–2,

[6] See Martin, Fanny, McEwan, Dorothea, Tatman, Lucy eds, *Cymbals and Silences: Echoes from First European Women's Synod* (London: Sophia Press, 1997); Ladner, Gertraud, Morer, Michaela eds, *Frauen Bewegen Europa: Die Erste Europäische Frauen-synode – Anstöße zue Veränderung* (Thaur, Druck und Verlagshaus, Thaur, 1997).

[7] 'Wells for India' was founded in 1987 by my husband, Dr Nicholas Grey, and a Gandhian friend, Dr Ramsahai Purohit.

women no longer have to walk several miles a day into the desert to find new wells, new possibilities open up: job creation, medical care, children's education, reforestation projects all play their part in the 'greening of the desert'. It is something I have begun to see as a Resurrection story happening before my eyes. But what I want to relate here is how, one day, our group returned from the villages to meet a group of local prostitutes. They, too, participated in the Resurrection story: they came to the well and learnt of the possibilities for their children's education in the project's kindergarten. But the new life went further: they begged us to set up a Children's Home and take responsibility for these little girls so that they could be saved from their mothers' fate. On this particular afternoon we met about thirty women, their children, and (to our surprise) the men with whom they lived, who controlled them and lived on their earnings. It was not something for which we were prepared. The group had come to support a straightforward water project and here they were in a tangled web, whose social roots were only half-understood. Our friend Ramsahai, co-founder of 'Wells for India', sat Gandhi-like on the floor, hearing their stories. Horrifying stories of little girls being kidnapped from mountain villages and separated from their parents at a very early age. Both he (who looked just like Jesus talking to prostitutes and sinners) and our group were close to tears and we felt that we could not refuse to support this project. By the end of the encounter we saw that to help the women meant helping the men. They, too, were caught in the web of poverty and hopelessness.[8]

What I learn for prophetic community from these images, is first, the need to move out of comfortable situations, face the truth of the lives of poor people and make the connections between power structures and the survival of poor women – and men. Joan Chittester's Peace Train journey showed her that there is not even a word in Russian for domestic violence. For battered women with no economic means and nowhere to go because of housing

[8] Now, two years later, a Home has been set up for thirty of these children, boys as well as girls. We have done this as a sign that there is hope, that prostitution is not to be tolerated, and that a different future is possible for the children. Yet it is a fragile hope, beset with many obstacles.

shortage, the only option is to stay in the same room as the perpetrator of the violence.[9] That is truly dwelling in the Dark Night of fear and no hope. Secondly, the power of solidarity is the basis for transformative action; and this, in the power of the prophetic Spirit, is the way to challenge and tear down the dominating and death-dealing powers which hold injustice in place. Thirdly, the prophetic spirit urges us into building community far beyond existing barriers and parameters, as I found in Rajasthan and as the European Synod found in Gmünden, when Muslim women asked us to replace the word Church with 'faith-community' in such a way that Islam would be included. One small step . . . And finally, the prophetic community consists of women *and* men: disordered relations affect us both and the way forward has to be discovered together, even if the journeys of conversion will be different.

These images all point to the kind of prophetic heart of community that we seek. First, we need a community which sees, hears and imagines differently. A community which is not afraid to confess either its vulnerability or its being claimed by the yearning (eros) of God, the passion of God for just relation, for transforming justice, will engage in the kind of listening, the hearkening, *cor ad cor loquitur,* of which Etty Hillesum spoke.[10] It will be possessed by what Adrienne Rich called 'a wild patience',[11] a spirituality of resistance which both refuses the present reality as inevitable and envisions life-giving alternatives of reconciliation, peace and justice. This is, of course, a reclaiming of the very biblical notions of 'seeing' ('Do you see, Son of Man, do you see'), of hearing, and of envisioning the Peaceable Kingdom in texts such as Isaiah 11. It is what Walter Brueggeman calls the 'counterworld of evangelical imagination'.[12]

But it is reclaiming these as dimensions of community life-style. The metaphor of the ear has become very important in

[9] Chittester, *Beyond Beijing,* op. cit., pp. 15–16.
[10] See chapter 1.
[11] See Adrienne Rich, *A Wild Patience has Taken me thus Far*, op. cit.
[12] Walter Brueggeman, *The Bible and Postmodern Imagination* (London: SCM, 1993), chapter 2.

Feminist Theology, as the insistence on both listening to marginalised groups and 'hearing into speech' the unarticulated stories of anguish are at the heart of the liberation process. There is a Rabbinic story which emphasises how listening is a crucially important activity for God. Two Rabbis died and went to Heaven, complaining loudly to God about their congregations, 'Lord, they wouldn't listen.' 'Go away,' said God, 'I have sunk my hearing in the deafness of humankind.' For this listening process to be prophetic, what is needed is both prophetic anger and prophetic imagination (already, in chapter 2, with reference to Nelson Mandela, I have alluded to the need to imagine alternatives to revenge and destruction).

But anger is problematic in Christian theology. Even though we pay lip-service to Jesus's righteous anger in overturning the tables of the money changers in the Temple, anger as a force for change is under-used in the praxis of community life, because meekness and the endurance of suffering have had pride of place and have been closely linked with essentialising notions of 'the feminine'. Another difficulty is that it is almost impossible in our imaginations to separate anger over injustice which is the result of aggression from anger which turns into hatred and violence (and there is a crying need to help abusive and violent men to handle aggression in non-destructive ways). In an eloquent article, 'The Power of Anger and the Work of Love', the ethicist Beverley Harrison shows how anger is a necessary response to the weight of innocent suffering and can fuel the struggle for justice.[13] In many cases where women have suffered abuse, instead of anger there is guilt, shame and a worsening depression which can lead to alienation, bitterness and suicide. Anger can put a person in touch with energy – but it is *community* anger in which I am interested, community anger which in compassionate solidarity cries 'Enough is enough' and turns this anger into action for justice.

But how do we awaken the prophetic imagination in minds, souls and hearts which have become so fragmented by the break-

[13] Beverley Harrison, 'The Power of Anger and the Work of Love', in Carol Robb, ed., *Making the Connections* (Boston: Beacon 1986); originally in *Union Seminary Quarterly Review* 36 (Supplement 1981).

down of community, whose thinking is dualistically opposed to feeling, and where the pornographic forms of eros afflict a society whose psychic imagination is diseased? In a society which suffers communally, like the boy Kay in Hans Andersen's story, 'The Snow Queen', from the fragment of glass which froze his heart and forced him to lack any warmth of reaction to his childhood friend Gerda – or to any human being?[14]

Walter Brueggeman insists that the community already operates out of a powerful memory, 'a memory that affirms that our past has originated through and been kept for us by a faithful, sovereign God who calls into being things that do not exist (Rom. 4.17)'.[15] It is no wonder, he says, that we are fearful and restless, because 'The world does not depend on us, and the world is not available to us. It is out beyond us in God's wisdom. It mocks our pitiful efforts at control, mastery and domination.'[16] Somehow, in our inability to accept that we are not in control, the dimension of the tragic is born (as chapter 3 explored). And yet, the community which has not lost its dangerous memory, which continually recalls its origins, has also retained its power to dream great dreams. 'Unlike the claims of a consumer society', says Brueggeman, 'the community operates with a powerful vision, a vision that affirms that the future is not yet finished. God has a powerful intention and resolve to bring us to a wholeness not yet in hand' (ibid.).

The power to remember with a subversive memory which stands in judgement over the dominant culture, and the power

[14] Hans Andersen, 'The Snow Queen' in Andersen's *Fairy Tales*.

[15] Brueggeman, op. cit., p. 29. 'Dangerous memory' or subversive memory has long been recognised as a tool by Liberation Theology. I wrote in *The Wisdom of Fools*, op. cit., p. 116: 'dangerous memory for the oppressed group', as Sharon Welch following Jean-Baptist Metz wrote, 'is the dangerous memory of freedom': 'this memory leads Christianity to a critique of what is commonly accepted as plausible; dangerous memory leads to political action. Dangerous memories fund a community's sense of dignity; they inspire and empower those who challenge oppression. Dangerous memories are a people's history of resistance and struggle, of dignity and transcendence in the face of oppression.' (Quotation from Sharon Welch, *A Feminist Ethic of Risk* (Minneapolis: Fortress, 1990), pp. 154–5).

[16] Ibid., p. 36.

to imagine and dream alternative visions of self and world, are at the prophetic heart of *ecclesia*. 'Imagine a world' (writes Brueggeman),

> no longer a closed arena of limited resources and fixed patterns of domination, no longer caught in destructive power struggles, but able to recall that lyrical day of creation when the morning stars sang for joy. . . .The world and all its socio-economic, political processes are placed between wondrous origin and full restitution. (p. 51)

If philosophy and theology have lost their prophetic, imaginative heart, perhaps a way back is through listening to poets, musicians and artists? (This is the argument of Robert Murray in, for example, *The Cosmic Covenant*.)[17] And surely, in this privatised society where most communication happens through TV advertisement or the Internet, the Church could offer a place for this to happen through a revitalisation of worship/liturgy, and in particular through a rediscovery and renewal of sacramentalism?

I would like to explore two examples of this. In full awareness of the tensions between the mystical Dark Night, tragedy, a spirituality of attentiveness, of waiting in hope, and the need for the community's prophetic action for change, I take what appear to be the two demonic faces of our culture – an unstoppable consumerism and the logic of violence. It is the combination of these two which provides the urgent motivation for redemption as 'gathering the fragments' and the recovery of the prophetic heart.

'I consume, therefore I am' and the renewal of community

Consumption I understand as the way we human beings use the resources of the earth to satisfy our needs and desires. Consumerism I understand as the public face of the prevailing defining ethic of our society. Here I do not intend to beguile or shock with statistics about the rich North consuming the lion's share of the earth's resources with consequences like

---

[17] Robert Murray, *The Cosmic Covenant* (London: Sheed & Ward, 1993).

reducing millions of poor Indians to living on pavements or turning vast tracts of formerly fertile earth to desert. There are many places to go for those.[18] The plan here is to explore Christian worship, in its identity as the activity of the gathered community, as a resource to stimulate community into the recovery of prophetic action.

But three problems need tackling. The first is the fact already alluded to several times, that consumerism actually constitutes the identity of the postmodern man and woman. We have become defined as fully human in so far as we are able to satisfy our desires by what we can buy and consume. Gandhi's maxim, 'Enough for each man's need, but not for each man's greed', is a despised proverb in the continual frenzy of whipping up our compulsive desires for ever more objects, clothes, cars, varieties of food and drink (usually out of season, imported from some poor country and produced in exploitative conditions). So it is not even being in employment, or being young, which constitutes the identity of the postmodern person. It is being in either the (increasingly) small category of people who earn the kinds of salary to promote and stimulate excessive consumerism, or among those who possess inherited money and power to flaunt the same money-ocracy.

But, secondly, which is not always realised, the reason why consumerism has hijacked our identities so totally is that this happens at the level of our psyches and our imaginations (hence the call for the prophetic imagination to resist and keep alternatives alive). Do we not see that the centres of consumerism, the great shopping malls, function as parodies of our cathedrals and centres of worship? They are usually at the edge of urban centres, attracting a car-mobile population – and therefore difficult for poor and elderly people to reach. Their architecture parodies the great cathedrals: have you not noticed the towers and spires of 'St Tesco's' and 'Holy Waitrose'? In a manner unnoticed by us, our perambulations around the aisles of the supermarkets parody

---

[18] For example, Rosemary Ruether, *Gaia and God* (San Francisco: Harper & Row, 1993), chapter 4, 'Narratives of Destruction'; Roger Gottlieb ed., *This Sacred Earth: Religion, Nature, Environment* (New York & London: Routledge, 1996).

ancient liturgies: the Word of consumerism is proclaimed, seductively and repetitively; the music of the adverts seduces our senses, along with the invitation to eat, drink, taste – all the time stimulating our desires for sensations, objects and fantasy shapes of our very selves. And, as Ian Linden, the General Secretary of CIIR, once said: 'the click of the till is the great sacramental act of today'. It seals our active membership in today's worship of consumerism. But in the case of the shopping malls, at least the people we meet are still real people; embodied encounters are still possible, and there *is* a real argument that wherever people are, that is where Christian community should begin. On the other hand, if encounter happens exclusively – as it increasingly does – on the Internet – then disembodiment and virtual reality have the upper hand. And there is no control.

Thirdly, this hijacking of the public imagination happens at a time when Christian liturgies almost seem to have lost their power to engage the whole person, mind, body and heart. Where is the power to stimulate wonder in creation, adoration, compassion and community responsibility for what is happening to creation? The cosmologist Brian Swimme recalls the ancient cultures where people gathered to tell the stories of being initiated into the mysteries of the universe.[19] This, he says, is not simply a question of scientific information about the universe – we have an overplus of that. It is initiating young people into a sense of awe, wonder, connectedness and responsibility for the sacredness of existence. Sadly, the caves of revelation today are mostly the darkened rooms where children imbibe the consumerist advertisements of today's media gurus and prophets.

What then are the key elements of a creation theology which will nurture prophetic action springing from a gathered community aware that consumerism is the disease which has hijacked our energies for de-creation, for blocking the divine creative energies and God's intention that all should share the Messianic feast? I name seven steps:

---

[19] Brian Swimme, *The Heart of the Universe* (video).

1. The way to tackle consumerism is to realise that we do hold the power of choice and the power to resist. The media wins because we let it. But it is as a community that we can be most effective in naming these choices for a sustainable level of consumption.

2. We need to recover and celebrate the connections between the sacramental symbolism of water, bread, wine, salt and their full ecological, material, economic and political dimensions. Charles Dickens, in *A Tale of Two Cities*[20] described this perceptively when he opened his story with the famous words, 'It was the best of times, it was the worst of times' and with a burst wine barrel in a small French village. For one glorious day the wine ran free for the poor, oppressed peasants – and meanwhile, in Paris, the blood of the aristocrats poured from the guillotine into the gutters: wine/blood/death/joy/violence – Dickens leaves us in no doubt as to the relevance of sacramental symbolism to life and death in society.

3. Our community memory enshrines sacred traditions which kept alive wonder and reverence for created realities; as well as the sacramental, there are the sabbath traditions of blessing, the covenant tradition, as well as mystical awareness. In the Russian Orthodox worship there has always been a fidelity to the centrality of liturgical experience as the heart of community. This was and is the mystical theology of the whole community. It is time to recover this as an explicit critique on consumerism.

4. At the same time, recovering connection with the processes of nature – from the cycle of birth and death to the daily rising and setting of the sun and the coming of rain just in time to save the crops – means that we experience these events at the core of our

---

[20] Charles Dickens, *A Tale of Two Cities* (London: Chapman & Hall, The Biographical Edition, XV), p. 1: 'It was the best of times, it was the worst of times, it was the age of wisdom, it was the epoch of belief, it was the epoch of incredulity, it was the season of Light, it was the season of Darkness, it was the spring of hope, it was the winter of despair, we had everything before us, we had nothing before us, we were all going direct to heaven, we were all going the other way.'

being. We accompany the suffering of the earth and express it through prophetic lament over loss, destruction and tragedy.

5. We proclaim eucharistic lifestyle[21] as the praxis of community. This is connecting the heart of eucharistic thanksgiving, the justice of its actual celebration, with the reality of the relationships actually being lived out in the community and its lifestyle.

6. All this calls for a renewed understanding of *sacrifice*. Ian Bradley, in *The Power of Sacrifice*,[22] has already called for the 'costly praxis of self-giving' as an explicit response to the exclusive focus on self-affirmation and self-indulgence (which of course are the fodder for consumerism). Building on this (but mindful that the call for sacrifice has often condoned unjust suffering, been blind to the suffering of women and underpinned an unhealthy spirituality where sanctity is equated with pain), sacrifice needs to be earthed in its primary meaning of 'making sacred'. But it needs to flow from its liturgical setting as the praxis of wonder, reverence, simplicity and joy in creation which hopes for the transfiguration of the whole cosmos.

7. Finally, the praxis of sacrifice will not be taken on board as communitarian ethic without compassionate solidarity with the suffering of all earth creatures and the poor communities whose survival is so intertwined with it. This is exactly the urging of the Spirit on whom we call liturgically to bless our offering. The praxis of sacrifice means solidarity and prophetic action beyond the constrictions and boundaries of our blinkered perceptions. It means being willing to move out of safety, familiar attachments and convictions to come on board – like Joan Chittester on her Peace Train – a global movement embodying an ethic which is life-giving

---

[21] A range of books and movements already exist, for example, Ronald Sider's *Rich Christians in an Age of Hunger*; Jim Wallis and the Sojourner community in Washington; Celtic Spirituality; John Taylor's *Enough is Enough*; Schumacher's *Small is Beautiful*.

[22] Ian Bradley, *The Power of Sacrifice* (London: Darton, Longman & Todd, 1995).

in the widest sense. In this sense we turn the old concept of sacrifice on its head: it is not altruism, repression of desire, self-denial which is the wellspring, but rather the eros of which Hadewych and the mystics spoke. The object of our yearning is transfiguration, renewal of the cosmos. Our Augustinian hearts are ever restless, set on fire for creation's renewal . . .

Surviving a culture of violence

In this last section I shall show how the heart of prophetic action needs to focus on the transformation of a culture of violence, and how here, too, liturgy has a function. If consumerism has become the public expression of contemporary identity, as I have been arguing throughout, violence is the unwritten contract on which society is constructed. The work of René Girard is so well known as not to need repeating:[23] put simply, violence keeps our society going; it is its hidden foundation. One chilling anecdote makes this clear. An American journalist, Janny Scott, who analysed the phenomenon of mob violence in the Rodney King beating in Los Angeles, wrote in a subsequent article, describing the execution of a murderer:

> The scene outside Florida State Prison at the 1989 execution of serial killer Theodore Bundy was one of the wildest. Parents brought children, men brought wives. Hundreds of reporters camped out in a pasture. It was like a tailgate party, someone said. Or Mardi Gras.[24]

When she asks herself why there is this fascination with violence, the answer she gives is that the execution is a brutal act, but a brutal act done in the name of civilisation (ibid.). As Gil Baillie wrote,

[23] René Girard, *The Things Hidden before the Foundation of the World* (Stanford University Press, 1987); *Violence and the Sacred* (John Hopkins University, 1975).
[24] Janny Scott, *Santa Rosa Press Democrat*, 19 April 1992. Cited in Gil Bailie, *Violence Unveiled: Humanity at the Crossroads* (New York: Crossroad, 1995), pp. 78–9.

> If we humans become too morally troubled by the brutality to revel in the glories of civilisation made possible by it, then we will simply have to reinvent culture. This is what Paul sensed when he declared the old order to be a dying one (1 Cor. 7.31). (Ibid.)

If civilisation rests on violence, how can we turn this around? A clue was given in the Costa Rica dialogue of women theologians in December 1994. Already in chapter 1 I cited Chung Hyun Kyung's keynote speech, 'Your comfort versus my death' and its story of the Korean 'comfort woman', Soo Bock.[25] I told how, almost in despair at some point, Soo Bock made the decision to eat in order to survive. It is this decision to eat on which I want to focus here. After a journey back from the shame and humilation, Soo Bock is now married and works for reconciliation. In Costa Rica the anguish, the Dark Night of the various forms of violence – military, sexual, ecological and economic – overwhelmed all participants; it was only through ritual that hope of healing was kept alive. And in our final ritual we shared tortillas – the basic food of Latin American women. Truly a eucharistic symbol, but also, literally, life-giving. Is it only with rituals of healing that violence, which has assumed ritual form in society, can be redeemed? Is this, finally, where the cross of Christ finds prophetic meaning as protest and resistance against violence, abuse and the suffering of innocents? Has the cross somehow, in a way we cannot fathom, plumbed the depths of the horror, the tragic, yet at the same time refused to let the murderer have the last word?

There is a terrible story of the El Mozote massacre in El Salvador in 1981 which tells of the death of a young girl, an evangelical Christian, raped many times during the course of one afternoon. Yet she had kept on singing right through her torture:

> She had kept on singing, too, even after they had done what had to be done, and shot her in the chest. She had lain there on La Cruz [La Cruz, the Cross, was the name of the hill where the soldiers carried out their killings] – with the blood flowing from her chest,

[25] Chung Hyun Kyung, 'Your comfort versus my death', in *Women Resisting Violence*, op. cit., pp. 129–40.

and had kept on singing – a bit weaker than before, but still singing. And the soldiers, stupefied, had watched, and pointed. Then they had grown tired of the game and shot her again, and she sang still, and their wonder turned to fear, until finally they had unsheathed their machettes, and hacked her through the neck, and at last the singing stopped. [26]

We are in the realm of great mystery here. We are witnessing to new experiences of transcendence. Soo Bock choosing to eat, the girl who dies on La Cruz and continues to sing, along with all children of Sophia Spirit, whose spirit sings in the midst of suffering, are turning aside the story of violence, and threatening the world with Resurrection.[27] The candles burning in this, the Dark Night, are kindled and kept burning by the Holy Ruaḥ of God. This I believe to be the great revelation for our times, that of the Spirit as Sophia, Wisdom, Hokmah. This, as chapter 1 hinted, was the fascination (although it remained undeveloped) of Thomas Merton for Sophia, a fascination kindled by such figures as Lara in *Dr Zhivago*. Yet he had, in fact, stumbled on an ancient Sophia tradition explored by such Russian Orthodox theologians as Soloviev and Bulgakov.[28]

Because God's Spirit is free, unbounded by restrictions of Church or indeed by human imagination, when active as Sophia, Wisdom, in the Dark Night of the human spirit, she is awakening us to forgotten or abandoned wisdom traditions of Christianity

[26] Mark Danner, *The Massacre at El Mozote* (New York: Vintage, 1994), pp. 78–9.

[27] 'Threatened with Resurrection' is a poem by Julia Esquivel reproduced in *Bread for Tomorrow*, ed. Janet Morley (London, Christian Aid, 1986), pp. 125–6; 127–8:

> I live each day to kill death;
> I die each day to beget life;
> and in this dying unto death,
> I die a thousand times, and
> am reborn another thousand
> through that love . . . (p. 127).

The source is *Threatened with Resurrection* (Elgin IL: The Brethren Press, 1982).

[28] See, for example, Brenda Meehan, 'Wisdom/Sophia, Russian Identity and Western Feminist Theology', in *Crosscurrents* (Summer 1996), pp. 149–68.

and Judaism, especially their expression in music, art and poetry. It is she who links us with ancient cosmologies to discover a vibrant presence of God in creation. A God moving us across boundaries to appreciate Spirit/Wisdom in other faith communities. This is glimpsed here in a passage from a North American Indian spirituality:

> There is a spirit that pervades everything, that is capable of powerful song and radiant movement, and that moves in and out of the mind. The colors of this spirit are multitudinous, a glowing, pulsing rainbow. Old Spider Woman is one name for this quintessential spirit, and Serpent Woman is another . . . and what they together have made, is called Creation, Earth, creatures, plants, and light.[29]

Spirit/Sophia in the Hebrew Scriptures is the very energy of God, bodied ceaselessly forth from the mystery of God's transcendence; as dear and familiar as the most intimate parts of ourselves, it is she who makes the connections between ritual, liturgy and the making of justice. Hers is the relational power I tried to articulate in chapter 2. She is the sustainer during the Dark Night. It is her practical wisdom – Aristotle called it *phronesis* – which breaks down the tensions between escaping the world and changing the world: practical wisdom, far from encouraging a body-denying spirituality, earths all ways of knowing in embodied, material realities, taking responsibility for them, and despises not the humblest of creatures as weaver of wisdom.

Conclusion

In this, the long travail of gathering the fragments of the brokenness of creation, it is the divine Sophia/Spirit who is restor-ing the prophetic and mystical heart to community, because she makes God known in the struggle for right and just relationships, in the fashioning of communities of integrity. Daring to dream, daring to hope, admitting our vulnerability, enlarging the powers of compassion – are these the fragile beginnings of redemptive

---

[29] Paula Gunn Allen, 'Grandmother of the Sun: the Power of Woman in Native America', in *Weaving the Visions* (San Francisco: Harper & Row, 1985), p. 22.

communities, fully Christian yet bursting the rigid boundaries of what we are familiar with as Christian? Is this where the Spirit is leading her children?

With this question, this dream and this image of a trinitarian God in dynamic, circular movement – the image of the three rabbits of Long Melford Church in Suffolk, and the three hares from Paderborn, Germany[30] – I dare to hope that even if the Dark Night is where we are, even if fragmentation is what we experience, yet, like the phoenix rising from the ashes, our communities, both prophetic and mystical in their counter-cultural response, are already fashioning a new integrity for contemporary society.

[30] These two images, one from England and one from Germany, may have some connection. The symbolism seems to indicate not only a God in ceaseless motion but, just as rabbits are supposed not to sleep, that God is ever watchful. There is an echo here also of the Eastern icon tradition of the perichoretic motion of the Trinity. It is also significant that animals have been used to image divine activity.

Bibliography

Allen, P. G., 'Grandmother of the Sun: the Power of Woman in Native America', in *Weaving the Visions* (San Francisco: Harper & Row, 1985)

Bailie, G., *Violence Unveiled: Humanity at the Crossroads* (New York: Crossroad, 1995).

Bowlby, J., *Child Care and the Growth of Love* (2nd edn.; Harmondsworth: Penguin, 1965).

Bradley, I., *The Power of Sacrifice* (London: Darton, Longman & Todd, 1995).

Brueck, K. T., *The Redemption of Tragedy: The Literary Vision of Simone Weil* (New York: SUNY, 1995).

Brueggeman, W., *The Bible and Postmodern Imagination* (London: SCM, 1993).

Buber, M., *I and Thou* (2nd edn.; Edinburgh: T. & T. Clark, 1958).

Carr, A., *A Search for Wisdom and Spirit: Thomas Merton's Theology of the Self* (Indiana: University of Notre Dame Press, 1988).

Catholic Bishops' Conference of England and Wales, *The Common Good* (Manchester: Gabriel Communications, 1996).

Chittester, J., *Beyond Beijing: The Next Step for Women* (London: Sheed & Ward, 1996).

———, *Woman Strength: Modern Church, Modern Woman* (London: Sheed & Ward, 1990).

Chodorow, N., *Gender and the Reproduction of Mothering* (University of California Press, 1978).

Christ, C., *Diving Deep and Surfacing* (Boston: Beacon, 1980).

Christian Aid, *The Gospel, The Poor and the Churches* (Report; London: Christian Aid, 1992).

Chung Hyun Kyung, 'Your comfort versus my death' in Mananzan, M. J. et al., eds, *Women Resisting Violence: a Spirituality for Life* (Maryknoll: Orbis, 1996).

Coakley, S., *The Three-personed God: An Exploration in Theologie totale* (The Hulsean Lectures 1992; CUP, forthcoming).

Cobb, J., Jr, and Griffin, D., *Process Theology – an Introductory Exposition* (Philadelphia: Westminster, 1976).

Conn, J. W. (ed.), *Women's Spirituality: Resources for Development* (New Jersey: Paulist Press, 1986).

Danner, M., *The Massacre at El Mozote* (New York: Vintage, 1994).

Dickens, C., *A Tale of Two Cities* (London, Chapman & Hall, The Biographical Edition, XV).

Dunn, M., 'The Church's Shadow Side' in *The Tablet*, 27 July 1996.

Eliot, T. S., 'East Coker' in *The Four Quartets* (London: Faber & Faber, 1944).

Erikson, E., *Childhood and Society* (New York: W. W. Norton, 1963).

Esquivel, J., 'Threatened with Resurrection' in J. Morley (ed.), *Bread for Tomorrow* (London: Christian Aid, 1986); reproduced from *Threatened with Resurrection* (Elgin IL: The Brethren Press, 1982).

Fitzgerald, C., 'Impasse and the Dark Night' in J. W. Conn (ed.), *Women's Spirituality: Resources for Development* (New Jersey: Paulist Press, 1986).

Foucault, M., *Power/Knowledge: Selected Interviews and Other Writings, 1972–1977*, tr. C. Gordon, L. Marshall, J. Mepham and K. Soper (New York and London: Pantheon, 1980).

Fox, M., *Original Blessing: A Primer in Creation-Centred Spirituality* (Santa Fe: Bear & Co., 1981).

Fulkerson, M. M., *Changing the Subject: Women's Discourses and Feminist Theology* (Minneapolis: Fortress, 1994).

Gately, E., *A Rich, Warm, Moist, Salty God* (Trabuco Canyon CA: Source Books, 1993).

Giles, M. E., 'Take Back the Night' in M. E. Giles, ed., *The Feminist Mystic* (1982).

Giles, M. E., ed., *The Feminist Mystic* (New York: Crossroad, 1982).

Gilligan, C., *In a Different Voice?* (Harvard University Press, 1982).

Girard, R., *The Things Hidden before the Foundation of the World* (Stanford University Press, 1987).

Girard, R., *Violence and the Sacred* (John Hopkins University, 1975).

Gottlieb, R., *This Sacred Earth: Religion, Nature, Environment* (New York & London: Routledge, 1996).

Grey, M., *Beyond the Dark Night - A Theology of Church* (London: Geoffrey Chapman, 1997).

————, 'Claiming Power-in-Relation' in *Journal of Feminist Studies in Religion*, 7(1) (1991).

————, 'Escape the World or Change the World? Towards a Feminist Theology of Contemplation' in *Your Heart is my Hermitage: Thomas Merton's Vision of Solitude and Community* (London: Thomas Merton Society of Great Britain and Ireland, 1996).

————, *Redeeming the Dream* (London: SPCK, 1989).

————, 'The Shaking of the Foundations - Again! Culture and the Liberation of Theology' in *Louvain Studies* 20 (1995), pp. 347–61.

————, *The Wisdom of Fools?* (London: SPCK, 1993).

————, 'Weaving New Visions: the Promise of Christian Feminist Process Thought for Christian theology' (Inaugural Lecture, University of Nijmegen, 1989).

————, and Opocenska, J., 'East meets West: a Dialogue', in *Jahrbuch of the European Society of Women in Theological Research*, 1 (August 1994).

————, Heaton, A. and Sullivan, D., eds, *The Candles are Still Burning* (London: Cassell, 1994).

Griffiths, M., *Feminisms and the Self: The Web of Identity* (London and New York: Routledge, 1995).

Hadewych, *The Complete Works*, trans. and introd. by Mother Columba Hart OSB (New York: Paulist Press, 1980).

Hammar, A. K., 'Transforming Power: Understandings of Power in Feminist Liberation Theologies' (unpublished M.Phil thesis, University of Lund, 1994).

Harrison, B., 'The Power of Anger and the Work of Love' in Carol Robb, ed., *Making the Connections* (Boston: Beacon, 1986); originally published in *Union Seminary Quarterly Review*, 36 (Supplement 1981).

Harrison, P., *Inside the Third World* (London: I. B. Tauris & Co., 1992).

Haughton, R., *The Knife Edge of Experience* (London: Darton, Longman & Todd, 1972).

Heidegger, M., *Being and Time* (Oxford: Blackwell, 1962).

Heijst, A. van, *Longing for the Fall* (Kampen: Kok Pharos, 1994).

Heyward, C., *Our Passion for Justice* (New York: Pilgrim, 1984).

————, *The Redemption of God: a Theology of Mutual Relation* (Washington: University of America Press, 1980).

Hillesum, E., *An Interrupted Life: The Diaries of Etty Hillesum 1941–3* (Washington Square Press, 1981).

Hogan, L., *From Women's Experience to Feminist Theology* (Sheffield Academic Press, 1995).

James, W., *The Varieties of Religious Experience: the Gifford Lectures of 1901–2* (Glasgow: Collins, 1960; Cambridge MA: Harvard University Press, 1980).

Jantzen, G. M., *Power, Gender and Mysticism* (Cambridge University Press, 1995).

Keegan, V., 'Highway Robbery by the Super-Rich', *Guardian*, 22 July 1996.

Keller, C., *From a Broken Web* (Boston: Beacon, 1986).

————, 'Power Lines' in *Theology Today*, 5(2) (July 1995).

Keller, E. F., *Reflections on Gender and Science* (Yale University Press, 1990).

Kitamori, K., *Theology of the Pain of God* (London: SCM, 1965).

Lash, N., *Easter in Ordinarie: Reflection on Human Experience and Knowledge of God* (London: SCM, 1988).

Lennon, K. and Whitford, M., eds, *Knowing the Difference: Feminist Perspectives in Epistemology* (London: Routledge, 1995).

Mananzan, M. J. et al., eds, *Women Resisting Violence: a Spirituality for Life* (Maryknoll: Orbis, 1996).

Matthews, F., *The Ecological Self* (London: Routledge, 1991).

McDaniel, J., *Christianity in an Age of Dialogue - Roots and Wings* (Maryknoll: Orbis, 1995).

Meadows, D. et al., *The Limits to Growth* (Washington DC: Potomac Associates, 1972).

Meehan, B., 'Wisdom/Sophia, Russian Identity and Western Feminist Theology' in *Crosscurrents* (Summer 1996).

Merton, T., *Conjectures of a Guilty Bystander* (London: Burns & Oates, 1965).

Merton, T., 'Day of a Stranger' (1962) in T. P. McDonnell, ed., *A Thomas Merton Reader* (New York: Harcourt, Brace & World).

———, *Elected Silence* (London: Hollis & Carter, 1949).

Merton, T., 'Hagia Sophia' in *Emblems of Fury*, cited in M. Grey, A. Heaton, D. Sullivan, eds, *The Candles are Still Burning*.

———, *Seeds of Contemplation* (London: Burns & Oates, 1949).

———, *The Climate of Monastic Prayer* (Spencer, MA: Cistercian Publications, 1969).

Miles, M., 'The Courage to be Alone – in and out of Marriage' in M. E. Giles, ed., *The Feminist Mystic* (1982).

Miller, J. B., *Towards a New Psychology of Women* (Boston: Beacon, 1978).

Moltmann, J., *The Suffering God* (1973, ET 1974; trans. R. A. Wilson and J. Bowden; London: SCM).

Moore, R. L., 'Mall things bright and beautiful', review of L. E. Schmidt, *Consumer Rites* in *The Times Higher Education Supplement*, 29 March 1996.

Morley, J., *All Desires Known* (London: Women in Theology, 1988).

Murray, R., *The Cosmic Covenant* (London: Sheed & Ward, 1993).

Nussbaum, M., *The Fragility of Goodness* (Oxford University Press, 1986).

Poole, M., 'Standing Again at Compiegne' (unpublished work).

Raymond, M., OCSO, *Burnt-out Incense* (New York: P. J. Kennedy & Sons, 1949).

Rich, A., *A Wild Patience has Taken me thus Far* (New York: W. W. Norton, 1981).

———, *The Dream of a Common Language* (New York: W. W. Norton, 1978).

Riley, M., *Transforming Feminism* (Kansas City: Sheed & Ward, 1989).

Rose, G., *Love's Work* (London: Chatto & Windus, 1995).

Ruether, R. R., *Gaia and God* (San Francisco: Harper & Row, 1993).

———, *Women Church* (New York: Harper & Row, 1989).

Sands, K., *Evil and Tragedy in Feminist Theology* (Minneapolis: Fortress, 1994).

Schmidt, L. E., *Consumer Rites: the Buying and Selling of American Holidays* (Princeton University Press, 1996).

Schwarz, W., Religious Affairs Correspondent, *Guardian*, 6 April 1987.

Shannon, W. H., *Thomas Merton's Dark Path* (revised edn.; New York: Farrar, Straus & Giroux, 1987).

Suchocki, M., *God, Christ, Church* (New York: Crossroad, 1988).

Swimme, B., 'The Hidden Heart of the Cosmos: Science, Religion & Cosmology', from Creation Spirituality Books & Tapes, Warminster, Alan Shephard.

Swimme, B., *The Universe is a Green Dragon* (Santa Fe: Bear & Co., 1984).

Tardiff, M., OP (ed.), *At Home in the World: The Letters of Thomas Merton and Rosemary Radford Ruether* (introd. by Rosemary Ruether; Maryknoll: Orbis, 1995).

Taylor, M. K., *Remembering Esperanza: A Cultural Political Theology for N. American Praxis* (Maryknoll: Orbis, 1993).

Tillich, P., *The Shaking of the Foundations* (Harmondsworth: Pelican, 1962).

Turner, D., *The Darkness of God: Negativity in Christian Mysticism* (Cambridge University Press, 1995).

Walker, A., *Restoring the Kingdom* (London: Hodder & Stoughton, 1977).

Ward, B. and Dubos, R., *Only One Earth: the Care and Maintenance of a Small Planet* (Harmondsworth: Penguin, 1972).

Ware, K., 'Through the Creation to the Creator' (Third Marco Pallis Memorial Lecture) in *Ecotheology* 2 (January 1997).

Weil, S., *Waiting on God* (trans. Emma Crawford; London: Fontana, 1951).

Welch, S., *A Feminist Ethic of Risk* (Minneapolis: Fortress, 1990).

Whitehead, A. N., *Process and Reality* (Cambridge: Macmillan Educational, 1929; corrected edn., New York: The Free Press, 1978).

Yeats, W. B., 'The Second Coming' in *Poems* (Variorum Edn.; New York: Macmillan, 1973).

Index